FACE YOUR FEAR AND WIN

BY RAPHAEL CHRISTOPHER

Important : General Advice Disclaimer

The information presented in this book does not and will never constitute legal or other professional advice.

No undertaking or guarantee, is given to anyone, the reader, third parties, to the entire world at large, anywhere in the world, whether expressly or implicitly in any way known to man, in the past, present and future, in any respect to the correctness, legality or otherwise, of the information contained in this book or any book published at any time by Testamark publishers or the author Raphael Christopher.

We reserve the right to supplement, change or delete any information contained or views expressed in this book at any time. We do not accept any liability for any loss or damage howsoever arising out of the use of this book or reliance on the content of this book by anyone, the reader, third parties, the entire world at large, anywhere in the world under any law appertaining to them.

By purchasing this book, you hereby agree to the above disclaimer and will not hold Testamark Publishers or the author responsible for any loss or damage howsoever arising out of the use of this book by yourself and any third party.

Acknowledgements, dedication & foreword

Without God, without my father and mother, Christopher and Grace Osili, without my wife, Jo and my princess, Chloe, my siblings, my Pastors Wendy & James Preston, our friends and you and everyone who has feared and won, this book would not be here.

I do not know a lot. I find the more I know, the more I realise how little I do know. You may read this book and not agree with everything in it. That is fine. You may know more than me. I am happy with that too. I know I am not perfect and will make mistakes. Today, tomorrow and all my life. I am comfortable with that.

Yet, my hearts desire is simple. It is to see you successful. Give you some tools to help you along your path of life.

Yet, I acknowledge the great debt of gratitude owed to you all and pray God's blessings be yours continually and may you grow despite your fears and may they never dictate to you ever again how to live your life!

May you live life free, joyously and enjoyably - just as God intended for you!

CONTENTS

CHAPTER 1

THE FEAR PROBLEM

It is timeless.

One world. Two forces. Billions of years. This problem affects over 7 billion people day after day and there is no end in sight.

Since the beginning of this world and the beginning of society itself, these two forces have controlled, dictated and directed every country, every government, every man, every woman, every child's reactions, actions, decisions and even the outcome of their lives twenty-four hours a day, seven days a week and three hundred and sixty five days in a year.

This pattern is repeated for thousands of years.

These two forces will continue to control, direct, dictate every country, every government, every man, every woman, every child's reactions, actions, decisions and even the outcome of their lives in every way.

To which forces am I referring to?

They are the forces of Faith and Fear.

The force of faith is a creative force. It carries with it senses of progress and positive possibilities. Faith, generally provokes a positive reaction but as with everything, there are exceptions to this general rule.

The force of fear is usually seen as a negative force that carries senses of negative possibilities and consequences. Fear, generally provokes a negative reaction. Similarly, like with faith, there are exceptions to this general rule.

In this book, I am primarily focusing on the subject of fear so I will only limit myself to this subject and visit the subject of faith in another book. However,

I would say here that faith is very important and we all need it.

These two forces are wired into our primary instincts and structures, into the very motherboard of our spirits, into our subconscious minds and memories, into our unconscious minds and memories. They can flare up without warning and in the most inexplicable ways and defies logic or reason at times.

And there are costs to having them which every person must pay.

The cost of fear, the effects and impacts of fear run into trillions of dollars and has cost billions of lives through the history of this world.

Fear in some way, directly or indirectly, has also been responsible for many, many deaths, diseases and sickness. Fear is also implicated and has some responsibility for unfulfilled dreams, marriage break ups, relationships hitting the rocks, disputes, murders and so on and so forth.

You can see that when you add everything up, the total cost of everything we have been paying, in terms of our time, lives, finances, mental health for fear dominating our lives is incalculable.

Now, think of your own life for a second. How much has fear cost you in terms of lost job opportunities, personal discomfort, sickness, worry about everything and everyone? What about the relationships you have lost due to fear?

Then multiply your conclusions by 7 billion and the result you get is directly the result of fear being experienced by all 7 billion people.
Think about the current Coronavirus pandemic. Think about the fear that governments and billions of people currently have regarding coronavirus.

Think of the face masks, the social distance rules, the self isolations, the lock downs, the quarantines and all the various other measures instituted by governments across the world in response to the coronavirus and many of these measures are driven by fear and there is no end in sight.

Now, think of the fears of 7 billion people combined together in one typical day. Think of the cost of one day's worth of fears.

Now, can you see the sheer scale and magnitude of fear?

It seems like a complex jigsaw. A picture, which we need to understand. We need to understand how we fit into that jigsaw and how the jigsaw fits into that big picture and once we see how we fit into the picture, we can be enabled to see the big picture clearly and our part and then be enabled to adjust ourselves to dealing with the forces of faith and fear efficiently and achieve the most harmonious results for our lives and for the lives of others, our loved ones and countries and succeed in living in that harmony every day of our lives. We would also be able to maintain that harmony until the day we depart this world.

If you accept and understand the theories and information, I outline in this book, I believe it is possible to achieve harmony and achieve harmonious results for all and if everyone did their part, easily the world will be a better place for all of us and we would be enabled to teach our children well and bequeath a better world to our children, our descendants and make our beloved planet earth safer, better and also be able to colonise safely the other planets and the entire heavenly galaxies and galaxies yet undiscovered.

Now to the burning question...

Can fear be faced? Can fear be defeated? Can fear be controlled or uncontrollable?

The answer is Yes, but as you will see, that answer is a multi-sided answer. You see, the answer to this age old and ancient question of fear and how it can be faced is quite simple but at the same time deep and profound.

This answer can be broken down into three facets.

1. The short answer is that fear can be faced.

2. The shorter answer is also that fear can be defeated.

3. And, the other answer is that fear can be controlled or mastered.

Good news, isn't it?

These multi-sided answers to the question of how to defeat fear draws from a unique combination of understanding of who we are, our makeup, drivers and a combination of sources of information, biology, psychology, wisdom, spiritual intelligence.

Let's start our journey.

Our road map for this journey in this book is in three broad sections. The first section deals with understanding current knowledge and thinking of how fear is understood. The second section looks at various types of fear.

The last section will show you how to face fear and win.

Every time.

CHAPTER 2.

WHAT IS FEAR?

Let us start with some science.

Generally, science is very important to our lives and has given us tools that has made our lives better. Tools like clean water, computers, internet, medicines, industrialisation and so on...

We are learning of new discoveries everyday. We are not yet there. There are more exciting scientific discoveries on the horizon.

Many definitions of fear abound. Some scientific. Some psychological. Some just common sense explanations.

Well, scientists cannot agree about the definition of fear. So, let us look into the biology of fear to provide some answers.

Broadly, there are two schools of thinking. One school says Charles Darwin, the father of the theory of evolution, whose book on the expression of emotions in man and animals published in 1872 is correct about fear.

Why do they say he was correct?

They say he is correct because he said that all human beings and animals have and share, to an extent, strong basic primitive emotions.

He identifies fear as one of these strong basic primitive emotions.

The other school of thinking disagrees. They say that fear is not necessarily shared by human beings or animals. They argue that fear is an individual emotion felt by the individual and this is not the same for animals to the same degree. They further say that the degree of fear is unique to the individual.

However, they both agree that fear is a both a naturally occurring emotion felt by humans and animals and fear can also be a learned behaviour that was not naturally occurring in the person or animal.

So, we can say with some confidence that fear can have being both, a primal, primitive or an instinct led behaviour and can also be a learned behaviour.

But we can also say with confidence that fear can also be learned.

An example can help to illustrate this. An example of primitive fear is the fear of the dark. Most newborn babies fear the dark. They cannot have learned this behaviour given they were just born. But we also know that for some people, even adults, that fear of the dark still persists in their lives.

We can then say with some confidence that the baby's fear of the dark is an example of fear being hardwired into our biological system automatically proving Darwin's theories.

But, at the same time, some adults fear of the dark is an example of fear that is learned particularly if they had suffered some trauma associated with darkness.

We can also say that this fear of the dark can also be learned again proving the validity of counter - Darwinian school of thought that fear can be learned behaviour.

The other example is the fear of fire. This is learnt fear. A new born child and to some extent a child up to ages of 1-5 soon is taught to understand that fire is dangerous and they learn to fear fire. This fear is learned behaviour.

One more thing.

The difference in both primitive fear and learned fear is only in the way the fears can come to be.

But, their effects, results and manifestations can be similar.

We know that these two types of fear can co-exist at the same time. In fact, many fears can co-exist within a person and the person can still be a functioning human being.

For example, the fear of dogs may be caused by a bad experience of being bitten by a dog. In this case, the fear of dogs is a learned behaviour. But the fear of dogs can co-exist with the primitive instinct where the person who is afraid of dogs has never been bitten by dogs yet still fears dogs but cannot fully explain why they are afraid of dogs.

When we say fear is a primitive emotion, we are saying this emotion is already wired into our genes when we were born and it is very much a basic instinct.

But a learned fear, is developed and has to be wired into our brains. It is not already wired. Remember, the example I gave of the learned fear of fire? That is a good example of what I am saying. The fear of fire was not wired into our DNA when we were born.

Still, both learned fear and primitive fear have very similar ways of operation and effects.

Let us zoom in on this process to explain it even more clearly.

Some writers categorise fear as an emotion.

By the way, have you ever thought about the word "emotions"? Do you agree that it carries a meaning of motion? We know motion means movement.

In the course of my many years of counselling people, it has become clear that emotions often move people from one state to another.

You may say that emotions and feelings are hardwired into your psyche to move you from one state to another.

I will illustrate.

Let us assume, at a certain time, you left your house at 7:30am, after a good night sleep for an important appointment for 9:00am. Your journey would take you about one hour so you had plenty of time to get to your destination.

If all things are equal, it would be fair to say that your emotional state at 7.30am would be that you are quite calm and relaxed maybe even optimistic. You may even be singing and in a good mood.

Now, you get into your car and start driving to your appointment and about 15mins from your destination, someone cuts you up in traffic carelessly and causes an accident and as a result, you become stuck in the ensuing traffic.

You missed your important appointment.

Now think, what could your emotional state be right now?

I would guess, you would be angry? worried? anxious?

All of the above or a combination of the above?

You see, your emotional state starting out that morning was that of calm and relaxed. Now, it has moved from the emotional state of calm and relaxedness to a state of anger, worry and anxiety.

Your actions, words and behaviour too has changed in the different emotional states.

Ok. Your emotional state has changed.

But, what changed it?

You will be correct if you said that your former emotions of calm and relaxed have now been moved and replaced by the emotions of anger, worry and anxiety.

But, what was the triggers that changed your emotional state? What was the drivers that drove your emotional state from relaxedness to anxiety and ready to fight or do battle at other drivers in traffic?

You would be right in saying that these emotions of anger, worry and anxiety were triggered by what happened to you which you had no control over.

But, did you have control over it? Could you have control over it?

Raphael's Principles:

To gain control of your emotions, first become aware of them and its motions and movements and how affected you are by them.

Whichever way you may look at it, your emotions have moved somewhere and have been replaced by a new set of emotions.

But, it is, still you.

It was still you that was experiencing the emotions of calm and relaxed.

Now, it is still you that is now experiencing the new emotions of anger, worry, anxiety.

In the future, moment by moment, those emotions would be replaced by another set of emotions and so it continues all the days of your life.

If the emotions linger or last for any length of time, I would call this a mood.

From this brief analysis, let us take away the following simple observable facts:

1. Emotions move you.

2. Emotions changes from moment by moment.

3. Emotions are temporary.

4. You are permanent.

5. Emotions are passing through.

6. You will remain.

Raphael's principles:

Emotions will come and go. You will remain. The fact that you will remain makes you stronger than your emotions and gives you the leverage to face them and win.

So, how are emotions made?

Science teaches us that emotions are mainly electrical pulses powered by biochemicals along the neural pathways of the human brain to make connections to certain locations within the brain. Depending on the strength of these electrical pulses and biochemicals, a physical sensation is then provoked as a response.

It is this response that we call an emotion. I use response to describe emotions because they are usually triggered by something external or by thoughts internally.

For example, a person may have a fear of flying. Their response of fear can be brought about by an external event, such as their boss requiring them to attend a conference for which they have to fly to get there. It can also be brought about by their own thoughts about the memory they have, when they previously flew.

If they have strong aversion to flying, they would want to flee from flying and decline to go, which may or may not have consequences for their ability to do their job well.

Alternatively, they can decide to fight their fear of flying by gritting their teeth and carrying on with or without any help.

This example, shows that emotions moves people to either fight the threat that brings the fear or flee from the threat bringing the fear.

So, what are the mechanics of how fear is made?

Fear is primarily accomplished through the brain.

Let's consider some biology.

It begins when the thalamus - a part of the brain which collects data from our senses.

This collected information goes to the sensory cortex and this is where the collected information is interpreted and organised and distributed for action.

It would be distributed to three areas of the brain with three different results.

Firstly, It could be distributed to the hypothalamus. The hypothalamus is where the decision to fight or flee from a threat is made.

At the same time, it would also be distributed to the amygdalae. The amygdalae is the name for a pair of almond shaped mass of nuclei situated in the middle and deep within the temporal lobes of the brain.

They are responsible for emotions, emotions making, emotions processing and decision making.

And at the same time, it would be distributed to the hippocampus. The hippocampus is responsible for memory and memory related matters and processes and processing.

This distribution of the information collected from the senses to these regions of the brain are aggregated together and cumulatively results in the emotions of fear.

These three regions govern the memories of fear. These regions of the brain also determine the reaction and response to fear.

For completeness, I need to mention that there have been many psychological studies showing that fears can be also evolutionary adaptations designed to keep us safe from existentialist threats, hurt or harm.

For example, the motivation personality school study conducted by J A Gray in 1987 describes fear in terms of one of 5 types - danger, evolutionary, novelty, social, intensity and learning. These categorisations, some say, is limited to only 5 evolutionary adaptations and these categories are not a description of fear itself but rather a list of what forms it may take in its evolutionary progress and as such this does not look at the biology of fear but rather at the evolutionary reasons for the fear.

However, the school of social construct psychology depicts fear as an experience constructed from our core affects and beliefs whilst the school of dimensional psychology sees fear as one location within a two dimensional world of reward and punishment.

The school of social construct's view of fear is seen as somewhat limited and does not explain the body's biology of fear and the school of dimensional psychology is only predicated on fear as it relates to the worlds of rewards and punishment with fear as a major factor in the decision of which dimension of punishment is being contemplated.

The psychological studies are, in my view, useful in adding to the body of knowledge that exists today in the consideration of fear and as such its usefulness exist in the array of psychological studies that shows that the fears can also be evolutionary adaptations.

There are many more studies out there however I have chosen the above example as merely representative of the views on the subject.

My approach in this book

There are many ways to approach this issue of fear and facing it and winning over it. Many have approached it from the biological viewpoint but that just describes the biological nature of fear but does not help in dealing with it and winning over it.

I could approach it from entirely the cognitive psychological point of view. This approach is also sensible and would make sense as this would explain the various facets of fear and can offer a proven way to handle fear.

Equally, I could approach from the clinical biological point of view which also makes sense as this would also explain some of the emotions and feelings we experience during an attack of fear.

Further, I could also approach it from the viewpoint of a hybrid of psychology and biological points of view and still it would make sense in explaining some of the mental viewpoints and techniques that are useful in tackling fear.

The fact is that these approaches are valid and do have cogent and proven benefits in dealing with fear however, in my view, having counselled hundreds of people over the years, they work but I have felt unsatisfied.

It seemed to me they do show the manifestations and the nature of the fear emotion and its triggers but do not necessarily show us the origin or source of fear. I felt they only showed fear's effects and triggers.

For me, they lacked the ability to unmask fear.

They are excellent in explaining the how, the why and the what of fear but they have not been able to explain the who of fear.

Please, hear me. I am not saying that the cognitive approach does not have merit or that it does not work. On the contrary, the cognitive approach works and it has been proven to work and I do recommend them as a solution for any sufferer of unreasonable fear.

However, I have considered many, many sources of information, literature and writings and whilst I believe they are effective yet I still felt something was missing and even though I did not know what that thing was, nevertheless I started searching for something that would make sense of the source of fear and who fear was.

I felt that there was still a missing link.

But what was this missing link?

After a long hard search over many years, I found what I was looking for.

I found it in the bible. Yes. The Bible.

Therefore, in dealing with the issue of fear, I shall focus on it and explain it from the understanding and viewpoint, provided by the bible because the bible provided for me, the clearest information I have found in relation to fear so far.

One evidence that helped convince me was the effects and the measures taken to halt this current global Covid -19 pandemic.

Studies after studies shows that the washing of hands and the concept of self-isolation, lockdown and quarantine are effective ways of stopping the spread of Covid 19 diseases and plagues.

These instructions, as far as anyone can prove, were first written about in the bible.

We are in the year 2020 and the measures our scientists and governments are using to tackle a global pandemic that has claimed thousands upon thousands of lives, came from the bible.

You can see this for yourself.

It is right there in the book of Leviticus chapter 13 and in the book of Numbers 5, these measures of self-isolation was instructed to be used in the treatment of leprosy and other diseases.

These were laws under the Laws of Moses which were the laws that governed the nation of Israel in their early history thousands of years ago.

This was confirmed by an 2002 article titled 'The Origin of Quarantine' written by Dr Paul Sehdev of The Department of Medicine, Division of Geographic Medicine, University of Maryland School of Medicine Baltimore USA

This information is confirmed by the WHO advice given to all in the current global Covid-19 pandemic and this confirmation can be seen directly and indirectly validating the information given by the bible for tackling these diseases.

CHAPTER 3.

WHY THE BIBLE ?

Why the bible?

I have researched into mathematics, biology, physics, chemistry, human anthropology, the earths history, no religion, different religions and ways of belief existing on this earth.

Whilst they are all very good and offered good solutions and sensible advice and structure.

I felt in my gut that one of them has to be right. But which one? They all sounds good, noble and very helpful to guide us on life.

Then I stumbled on a discovery. A discovery for me that changed everything.
This is the discovery.

"That the Bible is the best selling book of all time and Jesus Christ IS the most widely used reference point for the calculation of time for everyone and everything"

Hear me well. I am not saying there are no other reference point. I am only saying the most widely used reference point.

Let me explain. Bear with me.

This is huge.

So, in this year of 2020 and any other year, it is true that everybody, every man, woman, boy, girl, country, species, animals who dies will have a date of birth and a date of death.

Think about every birthday, every anniversary, every marriage, every job offer, every insurances, every licences, every food, every labels, everything - they all have a start date and an end date.

For example, in food products, we have the best before date. In car insurances, we have start date and end date. In tax returns we file to the Government, the period of time to which the tax return are stated to be. In our payslips, we have the date to which those payslips relate to, clearly stated on the payslip information slip.

Furthermore, our time is divided into units of time. Our days, months and years all follow a careful order and we all, rich, poor, government, country and everyone in between all follow and regulate ourselves, our actions, decisions by the details of time and the units of time.

The truth is therefore this:

Time controls, dictates and regulates all the affairs of mankind from beginning to end throughout all day and night. Time marches on remorselessly and waits for no-one.

We are born. We grow. We have children. We grow old and we die. The cycle of life.

Time rules this cycle. It cannot be defeated or changed.

Period.

But how do we measure time? We use two measures to measure time.

They are A.D and B.C.

The first measure is A.D. This is a latin word that means "Anno Domini" in medieval latin. This was translated as "in the year of our Lord". The full original phrase was *"anno Domini nostri Jesu Christi"* which means 'in the year of our Lord Jesus Christ".

There you have it. Jesus Christ.

This original phrase was shortened to 'Anno Domini' or A.D.

The second measure of time is B. C which meant "before Christ".

There you have it again. Jesus Christ.

How did this come about?

We know that the measures of time was introduced in the Julian and Gregorian Calendars.

The Julian calendar being the reform of the Roman calendar instigated by Julius Caesar in 708. This was gradually replaced and amended by the Gregorian Calendar that Pope Gregory X111 in 1562.

It is this Gregorian calendar that is used throughout the world and which governed all the affairs of the governments, countries, man, woman, girl, boy up till now, both now and for the foreseeable future.

This was astounding but what does this mean?

It means that all time, before the birth of Jesus - is represented as Before Christ or BC and all time after the death of Jesus is represented as A.D or in the year of our Lord.

Either way, Jesus sits in the middle of time. He is **the _only being_** used as a reference to calculate every body, every man, woman, boy, girl, country, species, animals date of birth and date of death. Jesus Christ is ***the only being*** who is used as a reference to calculate every birthday, every anniversary, every marriage, every job offer, every insurances, every licences, every food, every labels, everything that have a start date and an end date.

Jesus Christ is ***the only being*** who is used as a reference to calculate the dates and times for our scientific discoveries, our scientific experiments, our mathematical knowledges, our history and our jobs, working hours, our pay slips, our certificates in schools; our mortgages, books publication dates, contracts and the inexhaustible list goes on and on.

This is astounding.

Why Jesus Christ?

Why is the bible the best selling book of all time? The answer to me is pretty simple. Jesus Christ must have existed otherwise He would not be used as a reference point to calculate the time that rules all of us, all the time.

Then I asked myself some pretty hard questions.

If Jesus Christ existed then it must be true that Jesus was born and Jesus died. If this was true, which it is - what else does this prove apart from proving that Jesus did exist?

If Jesus existed, then does that make his claims and all that is written about him authentic?

I would say on balance of probabilities that it does. There are more evidence to say that Jesus existed than there are evidence to say that Jesus never existed. If he did exist, then I would be foolish not to accept him for who he is.

I searched everywhere to see if the Gregorian calendar or A.D or BC has been ever disproved either in scientific journals or other writings.

I could not find anywhere where the Gregorian calendar or A.D or B.C has been disproved.

Nowhere.

I looked everywhere.

Maybe I did not search enough. Maybe there are people with information that disproves this but as at the date of writing this book, none has been forthcoming.

The next hard questions.

1. If the bible is the book about Jesus and it is, then it should contain information about many other things that we have to face in life such as fear, death, sickness, tragedy and such.

2. If so, does it contain the information that finally umasks fear? Does it contain information that helps me deal with fear and win despite the presence of fear?

3. How can I access this information? What tools do I have at my disposal to help me? What can I do? Is there any mention of fear in the bible and

how does the bible approach differ from medical approach and are there contradictions?

4. If there are contradictions - what are they?

Let me say here that I am focusing only on the bible. I am not focusing on any other book or religion or belief.

Let me be clear. I am not qualified to discuss other books, religion or belief as I do not know enough about them to discuss them intelligently.

Let me say also, that even the bible I am discussing, I know only a little and do not know much either so there may be people who know more than me and able to correct, discuss, bring out other issues, points that I did not see or yet understand. I am happy with that because this work is only a conversation starter.

This book is partly to begin the conversation around fear and facing fear and winning every time. My desire being to put into the hands of everyone, a small tool that would help them to become less fearful, achieve their dreams and be a better human being, a force for good for their families, loved ones, their community and their world and our world for as long as they live.

If this book achieves this or even achieves a small spark, or even puts some good seeds in their minds and spirits or even educates just one person and helps them in their lives then my goal would have been accomplished and for that alone, I would be very grateful and it would have made all the work that went into this book very worthwhile.

CHAPTER 4.

FEAR

Definitions.

Let's start by defining what fear is and exploring our make up, the worlds in which we operate and the function of how we think in relation to fear.

Fear is defined in the English Dictionary as a noun. A noun is the name of a person, place or thing.

Fear can also be described as a verb. A verb being a doing word. An action.

This is so important.

It is important because it gives us clarity as to our understanding what fear is and how it operates.

Why is that so?

It is so because the more you know about fear, the more you will understand how it functions. How it operates. How it manifests. We all know the adage that knowledge is power.

Acquiring that knowledge is the key to successfully overcoming fear.

Now, we saw that fear is defined as a noun. Nouns' have a quality of personality and identity. It is ascribed a quality of living. A quality of being alive. A quality of being that separates it from being inanimate. It has the quality of being alive in the way that human beings are alive.

Just like a dog or cat is alive. In other words it is living.

In contrast to a dead or impersonal quality is given to things or situations that have no life in them or living.

Anything living has the ability of being able to interact with another living being. Anything dead has no such ability.

One of the salient truths is that fear being a noun is that this definition presents fear as a living being or thing and therefore can thus said to be something like a person that has life and can interact with other living beings like you and I.

I think on some deep level within everyone, there is some sort of understanding that this may be the case. When I refer to the deep level within us, I am referring to the subconscious mind within us. I liken this subconscious mind like the primordial world of planets and galaxies - a world within us.

Let me say here that research and our own experiences teaches us that we have two worlds.

We have the world outside us in which we all live in and we interact with this world through many means such as friendship, work, travelling, creativity etc etc.

We also have the world inside us. This inner world is a world that can be a world of wonders and amazement. It can also be a world of fear, evil and all sorts of chaos.

We have been given the tools and knowledge to create in both worlds. We have been given the ability and tools to fashion both worlds.

We have been given the vision to envision and bring into reality in both worlds, what we see.

Let us consider the outside world. We all interact with nature. The sea, the air, the flowers, other living beings and animals.

But we can create this outside world. We do create in this outside world.

We build houses. We build roads. We cook food. We plant gardens. We fall in love. We marry. We have children.

All of the above are positive or negative depending on your point of view. I prefer the positive point of view so I will say that the above are all positive, enriching and fulfilling.

But then, there are the negative side of creation of the outside world. The houses we build destroys nature. Plants and trees - giving us life giving oxygen - are destroyed.

We visit havoc on animals and plant life. The roads we build does the same.

The children we have may contribute to over population and the list goes on and on.

Such is the mystery of life.

The same good thing for someone can also be a source of pain for someone or something else.

Nonetheless, in both cases, creation is occurring in the outside world.

What about the world inside? Does this hold true of this world?

Well, the world inside is like a world of planets, galaxies and stars.

Everything originates from this world inside. Some like the world inside better than the world outside. We call them quiet. Shy. Introverted.

Others like the world outside more than the world inside them. We call them extroverts. Bold. Exhibitionists.

Everybody has their own world inside. My world inside is different from your world inside. There may be similarities in both of our worlds but they are never the same.

Not even in identical twins.

Everything originates from this world inside and then is manifested in the world outside. You can say to an extent that the world outside is a mirror of the world inside.

How does the world inside operate? The world inside you and me operates on three levels:

1. Pictures
2. Thoughts

3. Emotions

Pictures.

Very powerful.

For example, do not think of a pink elephant in a room.

What happens?

The chances are that you have thought of a pink elephant in a room. Maybe, a big strong pink elephant with mischievous eyes.

Possibly.

Any way, you did think of an elephant and with that thought of an elephant, you had a picture of an elephant associated with it.

Now, some people may have a picture in black and white. Others will have a picture in full vivid colours, painted and very colourful. Some may have a name for the elephant. Some may even construct a back story for their elephant. But others may just have the picture of an elephant and may begin to think various thoughts about this elephant. Where it may have come from? Others may remember a news series or movie they saw about an elephant. Some others may remember going to the zoo and seeing an elephant.

All of these activities, thinking, thoughts, pictures, back stories are all taking place inside the world inside of you.

Not in the world outside.

The world inside.

Do you see what is happening here? From the word elephant, you have created a picture. You have recalled movies. You have recalled memories of your experiences related to elephants and for some, you have gone further to create a back story for your elephant.

You can see also that you started to think thoughts as well related to the word elephant.

But, what are thoughts?

Thoughts are defined by the English dictionary as a noun. Not a verb. It means that they have a quality of living personality.

Unlike fear that is also defined as a verb. Thoughts are not verbs. Therefore if a thought is not put into action, it dies unborn. Whereas, fear compels action because it is both a living personality and has power to compel action as a verb - an action word.

Thoughts.

As you have seen and observed within yourself, thoughts come and they go. Some thoughts stay for a while. Thoughts have variety. From the noble thoughts to the silly thoughts to the downright rude and angry thoughts and everything in between.

Thoughts comes continually. They can not be stopped. Ever. Thoughts come from association. We have seen with my example of the elephant story that some of you thought, thoughts, associated with elephants.

Thoughts can also come from observation. It can come from what you see. You see a bakery with fresh bread. What thoughts comes to your mind? Well, you may fancy a piece of toast or sandwich depending on your state of mind.

See what thoughts came from your observations.

You are constantly arranging, rearranging your world outside because of your thoughts in the world inside.

Thoughts can be self generated by you such as where you are faced with a problem and you think about a solution for the problem. In this case, you are deliberately thinking and not just being a receiver of thoughts coming continually without your thinking them.

I believe that thoughts can be described as steady streams of consciousness. Like a river flowing into your world inside - watering the seeds of your life and causing them to bear fruit and that fruit are your actions and your words that can be seen and manifested in the world outside for all to see.

Emotion

The third component is emotion. If thoughts are like a river of consciousness, then emotions are the currents underneath this river of thoughts.

As we know from physics, water currents are found in every types of water, streams, rivers, seas and oceans however, no matter the type of water current, they have the same focus and intention. A water current is simply the rate of movement in a body of water that is or can be influenced by a host of variables such as gravity as in waterfalls etc and things like the slope of the land and such like.

However, currents are only ever of two types. Surface currents and deep water currents. Whilst they may be affected by the different variables mentioned above like gravity, how much wind, slope and geography of the land, the two types remain the same. The surface and the deep water currents.

Both the surface and the deep water currents are operating simultaneously in different rates, speeds and directions.

The deep water currents are like your deep unconscious emotions. You are not aware of them because they are unseen. Yet they determine by far the way the water flows. They determine the way you act in the world outside that everyone can see.

The surface current also determines how you act in the world outside but its power cannot match the roaring awesome strength of the deep water currents.

The surface currents can be pleasant and easily visible. But as you know, the currents on a lake is not the same as the currents in the ocean and sea.

Both of them are water.

Some people are like the lake. Placid and easy to get along with. Others are troubled, tempestuous like the sea, driven and tossed about by the wind.

When current swell and the water rises then the river bursts its banks. That describes the power of an emotion to force its way from the world inside of you to the world outside of you.

In the world outside, we see these outbursts and depending on how they make us feel, we call them anger, fear, worry, nasty if they are negative or love, kindness and mercy if they are positive.

The outbursts can be good or not so good. However, be aware that some of negative emotions can be good in certain situations. For example, anger can be good if directed to a worthy cause.

It is anger that children are dying unnecessarily that drove Edward Jenner in 1796 to research and find a vaccine for smallpox.

It was also anger that drove John Enders & Maurice Hilleman to create the vaccines for measles which has benefited the whole world.

But bad anger can be destructive. Many billions of people have been killed, since the history of this world, by bad anger.

You see, positive anger creates something good. Negative anger destroys everything.

In essence, thoughts are what makes you, you.

In Proverbs 23:7 (KJV)

" For as he thinketh in his heart, so is he"

In the background to this bible verse, we are told of a man who is stingy and miserly. He may say to you please 'eat and drink' but his heart is not with you. He is taking note of how much you eat.

Even though he outwardly, in this world outside, he seems genuine and generous but in his world inside of him, he is calculating how much you are eating.

Here, God is saying that that person is exactly what his world inside of him looks like.

You can see that thoughts are what makes you, you.

This is the foundation of all positive thinking and self help, self improvement, leadership, confidence building books, thinking, philosophies and movements.

This is all happening inside the world inside of you.

Every 60 seconds in a minute. Every 60 minutes in an hour. Every 24 hours a day. 7 days a week. 365 days a year or 366 in a leap year.

This is happening and yet you are unconscious of it all or if you are conscious of it, you are none the wiser as to what it is, where it is taking place or how you can understand it and work with it to create a better world inside you.

The entire point of this book is to bring these things to light these things that are taking place within you continually so you can see them and become aware of them and then that you can actually do something about all of them.

So, if you do not like the world inside, you can do something about it. You can create a new world.

You have the tools and all you need is the willingness and persistence.

Raphael's principles:

Fear is then simultaneously - a picture, a thought and an emotion of deep currents in the river of your being and consciousness.

That is why fear is very, very powerful but yet, we will come to understand that fear is not all powerful.

It can be controlled. It can be understood. It can be put to good use.

CHAPTER 5.

TYPES OF FEAR

Fear has many faces and many shapes. There are so many types of fears that it is impossible to categorise them all.

Mainly, fear has to do with fearing fear, fearing something or someone

The following 172 types of fear are listed below.

Forgive me, it would take 172 books to examine them in great detail but in this book, I am merely sharing them with you so you can see that fear has variety and many people all suffer from fear and you are not alone.

These fears are listed below with a brief explanations of each of them:

1. **Fear of God** - a fear where the person is afraid of God in a bad way.

2. **Fear of death** - a fear of not existing anymore.

3. **Fear of satan** - a fear of the devil and the harm and injury he can unleash on you.

4. **Fear of evil** - a fear of being harmed by evil people, evil actions and evil events.

5. **Fear of parents** - a fear of father or mother or step-parents and what harm or injury they can cause you.

6. **Fear of war** - a fear of fighting, a fear of the bombs, instruments of death and loss of one's life or limbs and loved ones sufferings and dying.

7. **Fear of the unknown** - a fear that you don't know what is coming or what to expect and what that thing you expect is really like.

8. **Fear of love** - a fear of losing control and being vulnerable. Vulnerable carries an expectation of being open and giving yourself wholly.

9. **Fear of wife** - a fear of your wife and what she would say, do or not do because she knows you and knows which button to press to destroy you.

10. **Fear of Husband** - a fear of your husband and what he would do when angry with you and his physical strength and loud voice that can frighten you with its ferocity and threat of mental or physical hurt.

11. **Fear of not being loved** - a fear that you are not lovable or being used by someone or not able to find a soul mate or someone who will love you as you wish to be loved.

12. **Fear of Aliens from other planets** - a fear that there are aliens out there who have a frightening shape and lots of scary sharp teeth, weapons powers that they are using to destroy the earth, you and all mankind.

13. **Fear of confrontations** - a fear that you do not like to confront people or be confronted yourself so you go to a lot of effort to avoid such and keep everyone happy.

14. **Fear of conflict** - a fear that you do not want to get into any conflict with anyone and you shy away from every conflict.

15. **Fear of poverty** - a fear that you will never have enough money to afford or purchase the things you really want or need.

16. **Fear of white people** - a fear of people who are white and who you think may hurt or harm you.

17. **Fear of black people** - a fear of people who are black and who you think may hurt or harm you.

18. **Fear of loss** - a fear that you will lose something very valuable to you.

19. **Fear of being emotional** - a fear of emotions and that emotions will make you look weak

20. **Fear of strong emotions** -   a fear that if you feel an emotion strongly, it may somehow make you look out of control and do stuff you would later regret.

21. **Fear of BAME people** - a fear of people who are black or Asian or Minority ethnic background and who you think may hurt or harm you.

22. **Fear of mixed race people** - a fear of people who are of mixed race heritage and who you think may hurt or harm you.

23. **Fear of your boss or employer** - a fear of your boss or employer who has power to fire you and demote you and stop your income.

24. **Fear of Government and authority figures** - a fear that the government is sinister and out to get you and do you hurt or harm.

25. **Fear of being an imposter in a top position** - a fear that you are not worthy to be earning a

good wage, being successful or receiving accolades and praise and somehow people can see through you and deem you a fraud and you will be found out by people and shamed.

26. **Fear of not being worthy** - a fear that you are not worthy of being liked, being successful or be given respect by people.

27.**Fear of not being liked** - a fear that nobody likes you and you are surplus to requirement and always the odd one out.

28.**Fear of letting go** - a fear that you cannot let go of something or someone and if you let go, you will never find something better or someone else.

29.**Fear of not being thought well of** - a fear of a very low opinion of you in people's minds.

30.**Fear of losing everything** - a fear that everything you worked hard for would be lost by you whether by your fault or someone else's fault.

31. **Fear of weakness or being thought weak** - a fear that you would be thought weak or see as a weak person.

32. **Fear that you don't deserve good things** - a fear that you think you do not deserve to receive any good thing or praise or have things go well for you.

33. **Fear that you have to be punished** - a fear that you have done terrible things and you have to be punished for the things that you have done.

34. **Fear of not being out of control** - a fear that you are incapable of being out of control. That you are too much in control and don't know how to let go.

35. **Fear of rejection** - a fear that you will not be accepted or welcomed by people or persons that you wish to impress and whose opinions matters to you.

36. **Fear of flying** - a fear of going into an aeroplane and flying over lands, seas and other natural terrains. You are afraid the plane will crash and you will die.

37. **Fear of spiders** - a fear that spiders are somehow going to hurt or harm you and you had better run away to save your life.

38. **Fear of open spaces** - a fear that open spaces are scary and somehow will injure you or harm you.

39. **Fear of closed spaces** - a fear that closed spaces are like coffins and you are trapped in them and you are likely to die.

40. **Fear of looking people in the face or the eye** - a fear that looking people in the eyes or face will expose your inner soul and those people will see you for who you are - a fraud or unworthy or undeserving person.

41. **Fear of heights** - a fear that you have no control and you will fall and break your bones and possibly die.

42. **Fear of driving** - a fear that you are trapped in a coffin like structure and you are out of control and likely to be involved in an accident and die or be seriously injured.

43. **Fear of ageing** - a fear that your skin and physical body are changing and those changes do not make you look good and you are then reminded of death creeping closer to you.

44. **Fear of being abandoned** - a fear that you are not worth keeping on as a friend, lover and therefore everyone leaves you and go with new friends and lovers.

45. **Fear of not being loved** - a fear that you will not be loved, that you are not being loved and you believe it is your fault.

46.**Fear of drowning** - a fear of drowning in water and losing control inside water that will then make you drown and die.

47.**Fear of injections** - a fear of receiving injections and that the injections would do damage and harm and cause long lasting pain.

48.**Fear of darkness** - a fear of the dark. A fear of anything in the night or a dark place.

49.**Fear of thunder** - a fear of the natural phenomena of thunder. A fear of its noise and that it would hurt or harm you and cause pain, injury or death.

50.**Fear of evil spirits** - a fear that evil spirits are present to hurt you, harm you and cause pain, sufferings, injury and even death.

51.**Fear of men** - a fear of men that men would be violent, and will hurt or harm you and cause you pain.

52.**Fear of LGBT people** - a fear of people who happen to be lesbian, gay, bi-sexual and trans or pan sexual. A fear that they would infect or affect you and hurt or harm you.

53.**Fear of women** - a fear that women are superior and able to use their superiority to hurt or harm you and you are unable to protect yourself against them.

54.**Fear of girls** - a fear of girls that they are somehow mysterious and superior and able to disgrace you and hurt you.

55.**Fear of boys** - a fear that boys are to be feared and are a threat and can hurt or harm you.

56.**Fear of children** - a fear that children are somehow stronger and threatening and likely to make your life full of pain.

57.**Fear of man** - a fear of what people may think or say of you and of what you are thinking or your actions and they can destroy you and make you look like a fool.

58. **Fear of water** - a fear of what is inside water or what lurks underneath a body of water and the fact that the water may be very deep and you would sink to the bottom and never be seen again.

59. **Fear of insects** - a fear of all types of insects being able to hurt or harm you and cause you injury and painful diseases.

60. **Fear of fears** - a fear of being afraid of any other fear.

61. **Fear of covid 19** - a fear of contracting coronavirus and possibly dying from it.

62. **Fear of germs** - a fear of invisible germs and their power to hurt you , cause you harm, pain and suffering and even death.

63. **Fear of sickness** - a fear of being sick and being around any one who is sick that you may catch what they have and become sick and in pain and suffering.

64.**Fear of embarrassment** - a fear of being shamed in public and made to feel small and foolish by other people for your actions, words and behaviour.

65.**Fear of body not being in proportion** - a fear that a part of your body is out of proportion and therefore sticks out in relation to other parts of your body.

66.**Fear of being fat or obese** - a fear that you would become fat or obese and people would not like you and would avoid you and not want to be seen around you.

67.**Fear of not being invited to social events** - a fear that you would be deemed not sociable enough or relevant enough to be invited to parties and social events.

68.**Fear of not being trendy** - a fear that you are not current or in fashion or on trend and therefore not relevant.

69. **Fear of being seen as weak** - a fear that people may see you as weak if you do not do certain things or act in a certain way.

70. **Fear that your face does not fit** - a fear that you would not be accepted because your face does not fit into the group where you are or want to be and this may cause you to over compensate or become who you are not just to fit in.

71. **Fear of people** - a fear of people and their behaviour towards you that may be threatening and potentially alarming and dangerous to your health.

72. **Fear of crowds** - a fear of a large gathering of people and you feel as if you may be caught under a stampede and not be able to breathe and feeling hemmed in.

73. **Fear of being alone** - a fear of loneliness, having no one to talk to and share your life and your experiences and comfort.

74.**Fear of failure** - a fear of failing in any thing, that you would not succeed in achieving your goals or objectives and you would be known as a failure.

75.**Fear of snakes** - a fear of snakes and their ability to harm you and inject poison into you that can cause you great suffering and death.

76.**Fear of blood** - a fear of your own blood or the blood of any other person that you may be infected and receive pain and suffering.

77.**Fear of ice or cold** - a fear that the ice or cold may kill you and cause you suffering and pain and if not taken care of, may even cause you pain.

78.**Fear of beards** - a fear of facial hair that it is untidy and contains many germs and such like and will pass on to you these germs and causing you pain and injury and the people who have beards are untrustworthy and have something to hide.

79. **Fear of chickens** - a fear that you would be pecked to death and caused serious injury and pain by chickens.

80. **Fear of pain** - a fear that you are going to suffer a great deal of pain and unpleasant feelings and sensations that it may cause to you.

81. **Fear of dying in a car** - a fear that a car is like a coffin and you would not escape death or injury if you are to have an accident or injury in a car.

82. **Fear of numbers** - a fear that numbers are scary and frightening and they are totally incomprehensible to you.

83. **Fear of maths** - a fear that maths is difficult to understand and this makes you feel nervous and wish to avoid maths.

84. **Fear of examinations** - a fear of sitting examinations or being tested by people and mind going blank.

85. **Fear of chaos and confusion** - a fear that there is disorder and chaos and that situation is no longer orderly and things in synchronicity.

86. **Fear of imperfection** - a fear that everything must be perfect or they are a failure.

87. **Fear of bacteria** - a fear of bacteria and the damage, pain and sufferings they have the ability to cause.

88. **Fear of ugliness** - a fear of not being attractive or desirable to people.

89. **Fear of mirrors** - fear that mirrors are evil and used for evil purposes and attacks against people.

90. **Fear of snow** - a fear of that snow is deadly and stops people movements and can cause pain and suffering and even death.

91. **Fear of books** - a fear that books can contain spirits and be an instrument of terror.

92. **Fear of gravity** - a fear that gravity is mysterious and powerful and if you are not careful, it can cause you real harm and hurt and even death.

93. **Fear of clowns** - a fear of clowns being masked terrifying and able to cause you hurt or harm.

94. **Fear of cats** - a fear that cats are dangerous and would hurt or harm you and you are not able to defend yourself.

95. **Fear of dogs** - a fear that dogs are dangerous animals and they are able to hurt or harm you without you being able to defend yourself.

96. **Fear of teenagers** - a fear of teenagers being people that something is happening to and who may hurt or harm you and there is little you can do about them.

97. **Fear of marriage** - a fear that marriage is a coffin and once you are in, you cannot get out and you have no way of escape and it seems like chains.

98.**Fear of knees** - a fear of knees, that knees are frightening part of the body and are can be used to perpetrate dangerous assault on you.

99.**Fear of speaking in public** - a fear that you are being judged to be no good by the people listening to you and you are tongue tied because you are afraid of people hearing your voice and thinking you to be rubbish.

100.**Fear of the sun** - a fear of the sun and the fact that it can cause cancer and other diseases and they cause serious pain and sufferings and even death.

101.**Fear of doctors** - a fear that doctors are looking to hurt or harm you and you will be used a guinea pig and end up with a deformity.

102.**Fear of room filled with people** - a fear that people in a room will resent you coming into the room and you will be judged on your looks and what you are wearing.

103.**Fear of colours** - a fear that certain colours are scary for you.

104.**Fear of the weather** - a fear that the weather is too powerful and can cause storms to destroy properties and equipments and will cause pain, injury and death.

105.**Fear of giving birth** - a fear that giving brith would cause damage and pain to the mother. A fear that child birth is dangerous.

106.**Fear of small things** - a fear that anything tiny or small has the power to inflict huge pain or be lost and cannot be recoverable.

107.**Fear of figures** - a fear that anything that is figure like has a capacity to hurt or harm you and may inflict serious harm.

108.**Fear of rain** - a fear that the rain can bring misfortune and pain and injury or damage and you are powerless against it.

109.**Fear of birds** - a fear of birds being able to hurt or harm you and you are powerless against it.

110.**Fear of horror films** - a fear that you are trapped and in a dangerous life threatening situation which may be caused by scary looking people or animals or inanimate objects like dolls.

111.**Fear of fire** - a fear that fire can get out of control and burn you and your property and bring you loss and pain and sufferings.

112.**Fear of halloween** - a fear of scary looking spirits and people with evil intentions out to get you and destroy you.

113.**Fear of school** - a fear that school is a threatening place and designed to punish you and you cannot get out of it.

114.**Fear of sleep** - a fear that you may go to sleep and never wake up.

115.**Fear of strangers** - a fear that strangers are harbouring evil intentions to harm you, injure you and even kill you.

116.**Fear of witches and witchcraft** - a fear that witches and witchcraft are real and are working to hurt and harm you and you are none the wiser.

117.**Fear of foreigners and immigrants** - a fear of anyone not a native born and of the same race.

118.**Fear of prison** - a fear of being labelled a criminal and sent to prison and having a criminal record which would affect your chances of employment.

119.**Fear of beautiful women** - a fear that beautiful woman are too beautiful, promiscuous and are unreachable.

120.**Fear of religion** - a fear that religion stifles individual behaviour and can cause fear and hatred that can bring death.

121.**Fear of handsome men** - a fear that a handsome man is too handsome and therefore unreachable and untrustworthy.

122.**Fear of the truth** - a fear that if the truth comes out and you are found lying, you would lose everything.

123.**Fear of promotion** - a fear that if you are promoted, you will not be able to do the job and you will be found out as a fake.

124.**Fear of being a leader** - a fear that you are going to be responsible for what happens to everyone and you would be blamed if anything went wrong.

125.**Fear of being afraid** - a fear that you do not want to be afraid of any situation in life

126.**Fear of being disliked** - a fear of being the subject of people's dislike

127.Fear that something evil is about to happen
a fear that an unexpected evil is about to befall a person.

128.Fear of misfortune - a fear that a misfortune is about to befall a person

129.Fear of speaking - a fear of opening your mouth and speaking in various settings and situations because you feel that what you may say may make you stand out and look foolish or make you look stupid in the eyes of your listeners.

130.Fear of time - a fear that you are going to run out of time and that would cause you harm and loss.

131.Fear of cooking - a fear that your cooking will not turn out well or be as tasty as others cooking.

132.Fear of eating food - a fear that food will cause your body to become bloated and big and you will end up being obese and unattractive.

133.**Fear of siblings and family members** - a fear that your siblings and family members are cruel and a terror to you and have caused you pain and sorrow.

134.**Fear of being bullied** - a fear of being subjected to attacks, injuries and harm by bullies.

135.**Fear of being a subject of gossip** - a fear that people are talking bad things and evil about you behind your back and these are affecting your reputation and self respect.

136.**Fear of being labelled** - a fear of labelled with a bad label and which makes you look bad and destroys your image in the eyes of people.

137.**Fear of ostracisation** - a fear of being exiled or left out of things socially or otherwise and you are not in the inner circle of those in the know anymore.

138.**Fear of being the black sheep** - a fear of being different from everyone and being humiliated because of it.

139.**Fear of race** - a fear of people from different races. You believe they will hurt you and harm you.

140.**Fear of loud voices** - a fear of loud voices. You are afraid that loud voices are threatening and which raises the possibility that you may be hurt or harmed.

141.**Fear of people standing in your personal space** - a fear of having people standing in your personal space making you feel uncomfortable and afraid.

142.**Fear of vulnerability** - a fear of not being perfect and having a weakness that can be exploited and can be used to cause you harm.

143.**Fear of sex** - a fear of sexual intimacy and thinking that sex is wrong and should not be indulged in.

144.**Fear of not being able cope with fear** - a fear that fear is overwhelming and you cannot contain or control your fear.

145.**Fear of going online** - a fear of online activities and that online is full of evil things and not a place to be trusted.

146.**Fear of the dark web** - a fear that the dark web is full of evil and a place to be avoided at all costs.

147.**Fear of being scammed** - a fear of being a victim to a scam where you lose lots of money to scammers.

148.**Fear of dirt** - a fear that dirt is harmful to you because of the germs and bacteria it contains and you feel that if it touches you, it would cause you harm and bring suffering and pain upon you.

149.**Fear of being followed** - a fear that someone is following you and their intentions are to do you harm and cause you suffering.

150.**Fear of noise** - a fear of loud noises that you feel may damage your ear drums and cause you headaches and migraines.

151.**Fear of strangers** - a fear of any person you do not really know well enough and you feel they would do you evil, and harm you.

152.**Fear of the police** - a fear that the police are after you and once they catch up with you, you would be subjected to suffering and end up in prison.

153.**Fear of gangs** - a fear of gangs that they will hurt you if you don't join them or stay out of their way or you do not do what they asked.

154.**Fear of being naked** - a fear of being naked and all your body being seen.

155.**Fear of being ghosted** - a fear of your relationship being ended suddenly without any explanation.

156. **Fear of being a snitch** - a fear of being labelled a traitor or judas and being subjected to harm, threats and suffering.

157. **Fear of being gaslighted** - a fear of being made to doubt your own sanity or state of mind by psychological manipulations.

158. **Fear of being called a Karen** - a fear of being labelled as a middle aged white woman who believes she is entitled to everything and demanding to speak to a manager to get it even though she is not so entitled.

159. **Fear of losing children** - a fear of a child dying before the parents and the unbearable pain that would cause.

160. **Fear of losing husband or partner** - a fear of a husband or partner dying before you and the unbearable pain that would bring.

161. **Fear of other men or women stealing partner** - a fear that other men or woman

would steal your partner and the suffering and damage that would do to you.

162.**Fear of approaching women** - a fear that if you approach woman you will be met with insults, contempt and disdain and made to look foolish.

163.**Fear of approaching men** - a fear that if you approach men, you will be met with contempt and disdain and made to look desperate or without self respect.

164.**Fear of being jilted** - a fear of being rejected by the object of your love during the course of a relationship and which will result in long term emotional pain.

165.**Fear of being photographed** - a fear of not wanting your photograph to be taken for fear it may be used for evil purposes.

166.**Fear of not having privacy** - a fear that your privacy has been compromised and your secrets are laid bare for all to see.

167.**Fear of indoors** - a fear of being indoors and it feels as if you are imprisoned within your own home.

168.**Fear of losing one's hair** - a fear that your hair are falling out and you will end up bald and not looking good.

169.**Fear of impotence** - a fear of not being able to gain an erection and make love.

170.**Fear of infertility** - a fear that you may not be able to father a child or fall pregnant and give birth to a baby.

171.**Fear of being cursed** - a fear of being the target of a curse and that somehow the curse will affect you and you are helpless against its power.

172.**Fear of incontinence** - a fear that your bladder and urine muscles may grow weak and you may start to leak urine which will cause you embarrassment.

173.**Fear of creepy crawlies** - a fear of all creepy crawlies as terrifying creatures that causes you fear and harm.

174.**Fear of the outdoors** - a fear of the outdoors and open spaces, a feeling of being not in control and there are so many terrors that could be lurking out there to cause you harm.

175.**Fear of espionage** - a fear that you are being spied upon and your secrets and work secrets are being extracted to use to harm you.

176.**Fear of defamation** - a fear of people saying things about you that are not true to others or to the general public.

177.**Fear of revenge porn** - a fear that your partner from your previous relationship that ended badly may share videos of your sexual relationship online as a way to hurt or harm you or destroy you.

178.**Fear of being lied to** - a fear where you are afraid that people are telling you lies and which will cause you problems and loss.

179.**Fear of being taken advantaged of** - a fear where your good nature and kindness is being abused by people for their selfish ends.

180.**Fear of losing money** - a fear of losing money that you did not have or that you borrowed and which will cause you pain and worry.

181.**Fear of losing good reputation** - a fear that your reputation would be soiled and you would not be respected anymore.

182.**Fear of losing good name** - a fear that your good name would be destroyed because of a situation or certain acts and words associated with you.

183.**Fear of being found out** - a fear of being found that you may have been lying or doing things that you shouldn't be doing.

From the above list of fears you can identify with some fears and you may be having these combinations of fear all coexisting together.

We can understand the above list.

Why?

It is because the object of the fear can be be easily identified.

However, there are some fears that cannot be pinpointed yet the individual feel they are there. In such cases, you may be able consider that fear and compare it to any of the fears on the above list and see which one closely matches the feeling you are feeling and that will guide you to be able to make sense of your fear.

However, the effects of the fear on human beings and animals differ widely in severity and behaviour.

You can have the same sort of fear but very widely varying physical, psychological reactions in the individuals affected by that fear both short term and long term.

This is why you cannot generalise how a person would feel when they have a particular type of fear.

You have to have them tell you exactly how they are feeling in order to understand how this is making them feel and not use your own experience to substitute for the other persons feelings.

We know that we human beings, myself included, tend to be in a hurry and are not always patient or sensitive enough to allow an individual enough time for them to be able to communicate their feelings without being hurried up or judged.

The above list of fears are nowhere near conclusive. The above list of fears are just a tip of the iceberg. There are so many fears not listed above. There are fears that has not even been labelled or described yet.

There are fears that people do not yet know that they are fears. There are fears that have yet to be diagnosed as fears medically or psychologically. There are fears that goes away and comes back. There are fears you cannot put a handle on, yet it is there. The list of fears are increasing as new knowledge emerges and more light shines on fears, shines on the human condition and identifies them.

Fears can be generation specific.

Every generation has specific fears that are peculiar to that generation. No two generations are the same.

Yet there are fears that are common to all generations. One fear that is common to all generations is the fear of death. But the fear of being a Karen is not common to all generations. That fear is common to this generation.

Another example is the fear of being online. This fear was not common to the generation that did not have access to online or the internet. Every generation had their own unique fears which arose as a result of so many factors and events but in looking at these fears, some of them, not all, appear to have arisen because of the advances and technology that has been developed and in the mainstream.

The example of the industrial revolution is a case in point. The advent of the industrial revolution with the sweeping changes it made to the life and the psychological well being and make up of millions of people, engendered fears of a different kind. For instance, many who had horses and carts now became afraid that they were being supplanted by the faster vehicles that was being built and people were no longer depending on the horses and carts to transport their goods any more.

You can imagine that and appreciate why they were afraid and unfortunately, their fears proved true.

That was unique to that generation.

The same can be said of this generation and the internet. Now, the internet is here to stay and many people are now turning to the internet to shop and purchase everything from food to houses and everything in between, many shops on the high street and in shopping centres are suffering low sales because people are now preferring to shop from the convenience of their homes and this way of shopping has many advantages for them.

The owners of the shops on the high street are now afraid of going out of business due to the increase in people shopping online. Indeed, their fears are proving true and we are now seeing huge swathes of the High Street shops are now closing down and household names going into administration due to lack of sales and business losses.

This is unique to this generation.

Fears are also mainly personal and I dare say, you would have identified several fears on the above list as fears that you may have had or still have or yet to have during your life.

The thing is, fear is unique to individuals. Fear can also be universal to a group of people and to the entire human race.

Fear can be unique to individuals. What you fear may not be what I fear and what I fear is not the same as what the next person fears or vice versa. Fear can be universal in that everybody has some fear of some sort whether they like to admit it or not nevertheless those fears are there. They may be hidden and hidden well yet the fears are somewhere hidden and there.

Fears can be admitted or kept secret. Many people pretend they are not afraid and they project a happy and brave face to the world.

Nonetheless, they are there. The sooner the individual faces up to the fears, the better they can tackle them and win.

As I have stated before, the clearest explanation for me, that I have found in relation to fear comes from the bible. I have no doubt that many will disagree with me immediately so let me say straight off that I accept I may not be right.

I may be wrong and I am never afraid of being wrong on anything. In fact, I am not the first and neither will I be the last person to be wrong about anything - both now or in the future.

In fact, I recall Galileo the scientist, who is known as the father of modern science stated that the earth revolved round the sun. He was placed under house arrest and even Copernicus and others who had said the same thing earlier than Galileo were vilified and discredited because it was not the conventional thinking in those days.

Were they wrong? No. Time proved them right. Today, everyone knows that the earth revolves round the sun.

The same happened with Louis Pasteur. He said diseases were spread by germs. Eliminate the germs and you eliminate the disease. He said so in the 1850's. He was ostracised by his fellow professionals.

Was he proved right? Of course, he was. Today, we have made strides in the medical field because of his theory and thinking.

Look at the reactions, Galileo and Pasteur received. Those reactions were from individuals and groups who disagreed with their thinking and acted out of fear.

On the other hand, we see very much the same applying to thinkings which were accepted and later proved wrong.

There is the theory of tabula rasa propounded by John Locke in the 1689 that human beings are born a blank slate and everything we then know comes from our experience and what we were taught.

But this is not strictly true because modern science suggests that our genes, DNA, family history, our instincts all play a part in our upbringing.

So, John's thinking was proved wrong.

Another person whose thinking was proved wrong was Einstein's static universe model. He thought that the universe was stationary in 1917 but the discovery of the dynamic relationship between red shift by Edwin Hubble completely showed Einstein's thinking of a stationary universe as not true because the Edwin Hubble's discovery showed that the universe is constantly expanding.

Again, time proved that the accepted thinking of Einstein in his static universe model was wrong in the same way that Time proved Galileo's theory of the sun being the centre of the universe was right. In both cases, the same time that proved one right also proved the other wrong.

Does the fact that time proved Einstein's theory of the static universe wrong mean that Einstein was wrong on everything?

No. Not at all.

Einstein proved right in his theory of relativity and his theory was also proved right by Professor Stephen Hawkins and has aided a more thorough understanding of the cosmos and helped in engineering spacecrafts and other devices that astronomers are now using in the exploration of space and which are increasing our knowledge of our universe.

So, if Einstein was afraid, would he have been able to propound his theories? I think not. The fact that he did not get things right 100 times out of 100 shows his humanity and show his uniqueness as a human being and shows that you do not have get right everything 100 times out of a 100 times to be a worthy human being. You can get it wrong and still be a worthy and normal human being.

In fact, no one ever gets it right 100 times out of a 100 times and no one will ever will, no matter what any one would have you believe.

It is only when we all work together as a team throughout the world, then we together as a team will be able to get it right 100 times out of a hundred times.

And fear is the single most powerful factor stopping this from happening - that is why I am writing this book to help you understand the truth about why we all need each other and why we all need to help each other and why we need all our individual talents and gifts and harness them together to make our world better, the world better and altogether a better place for us, our loved ones and our children and the generations yet unborn.

So, I may not be as intelligent as some people are. I realise there are people more smarter, more intelligent and better than me in every way, I am comfortable with this knowledge and appreciate them yet I also appreciate myself as a unique person whilst in no way denigrating anyone.

I also realise everyone will have their own thoughts and I do welcome them because the purpose of this book is to make you think, reflect and become aware of your fears and be equipped to help you win, despite these fears so you can be a successful, healthy and blessed person and be able to help others, your loved ones and your family and your community and their world at large so we all can make this world, our worlds, a better place for all. Back to what I was saying. I was saying that for me, for me alone, the clearest explanation and information on fear and how to win against it, comes from the bible.

I understand that to many people, the bible does not make sense or even give any great details but however, the question is - what if the bible is true?

We have already established form the A.D and B.C theory that Jesus Christ is real and true.

The bible is the book about Jesus Christ.

Therefore, the bible has to be real and true too.

As ever, to choose to believe the bible is an individual choice. A person has to choose, freely and unemotionally, that the bible is true.

It is an individual choice. Nobody has any right to foist their own beliefs on another.

A person can be convinced but that's not necessary. The person simply has to make a personal choice to believe the bible or not.

No-one can make that choice for you.

That said, let us come back to the issue at hand.

Fear has featured in many people, governments and societies lives throughout the centuries.

I had said earlier about the examples of Galileo, Copernicus, Louis Pasteur and others, I have spoken about the unique generational fear of industrialisation in the industrial revolution in 1800-1900s and the rise of online shopping in the 21st century, and the powerful positive and negative impacts it has had on the world and upon huge swathes of people, cities, countries and governments over the centuries.

You can see immediately how powerfully fear has motivated and pushed otherwise good people into acting unreasonably.

This same situation goes on, day after day in every walk of life, governments, families, offices, businesses, schools and all over the world.

Why?

It is because, as we have seen previously that fear is invisibly rooted inside the DNA of every man, woman born and yet unborn. It is wired into our primitive and primordial instincts.

As such, fear is very, very powerful. It governs nearly everybody in one form or the other, It motivates the rich and powerful. It equally motivates the poor and not so powerful. It affects governments, companies, families, institutions. Nearly everyone is affected by fear or the effects of fear.

Animals are also affected by fear but we do not know to what extent and whether it is to the same degree as a human being does however, the pervasiveness of fear is such that it is unlikely that anything or anyone in all of creation are immune to fear in some way, shape or form.

Psychologists call it the fight or flight instincts.

Fear has the unique power and force to turn something, nothing, anything, any one into a threat or weapon.

Fear can turn anyone and anything into itself and use that person, nothing or thing as tool to project itself against it's intended target with the objective of destroying its intended target or targets or coercing them into submission to itself through its ascription of itself and its powers to that perpetrating tool or person.

Fear is invisible. Fear is a force. Although it is invisible and cannot be seen yet its effects and impacts are visible and can be felt, seen and touched.

We see fear causing the current riots in America and people panic buying toilet rolls during the early stages of the Covid -19 pandemic all across the world.

CHAPTER 6.

FEAR UNMASKED

So, what does the bible say about fear?

The bible says that all those faces and shapes of fear like those I listed earlier, all boils down to one source. It all comes from one source. Only one source originates it all.

The source of fear is invisible.

Fear is a supernatural force.

Fear is a spirit.

The Apostle Paul told his son Timothy in the faith of Jesus, the following:

2 Timothy 1:7 (King James Version)

"...For God hath not given us **the spirit of fear**; but of power, and of love, and of a sound mind..."

Here, this noted Apostle Paul identified that fear is a spirit. He called it *'the spirit of fear'*. This gives fear its identity and its personality and characteristics.

So then, what is a spirit?

A spirit is a supernatural invisible being existing in the unseen world but which affects the physical world.

A spirit is invisible. They cannot be seen. They cannot be touched. But they can be felt in certain situations.

A spirit is supernatural. A spirit cannot be detected by any machine, software, equipment no matter how sophisticated those machines may be.

To put this in context, God is a Spirit.

In John 4:24, Jesus told his disciples that God is a Spirit and God is a He. We know this because Jesus said that those who worship *him,* must worship him in spirit and in truth.

We note from these words of Jesus that not everyone will worship God for Jesus said *those* who worship him. *Those* does not mean *all*.

Man is a spirit being as well.

1 Thessalonians 5:23 KJV:

*"...And the very God of peace sanctify you wholly; and I pray God **your whole spirit and soul and body** be preserved blameless unto the coming of our Lord Jesus Christ..."*

We see that man is also made up of his spirit, his soul and his body.

So, man's personality and make-up encompasses three worlds. The physical world. The mental & emotional world. The spiritual world.

Man's spirit contacts the spiritual world. Man's soul contacts the mental and emotional world.

Man's body contacts the physical world.

As we know, it is not everything that exists that we can see with our natural eyes unaided by technology and devices.

For example, we cannot see radio waves with our natural eyes. We cannot see certain spectrums of light with our natural eyes. We cannot see electromagnetic waves with our natural eyes.

We cannot see the Covid-19 virus with our eyes yet we see the devastation something we cannot see has wrought on our world.

We need special equipment costing in some case, thousands of pounds or dollars, to be able to see some of the unseen particles of energy.

Does the fact we can't see these particles of energy with our unaided natural eyes means that those particles of energy do not exist?

Of course, No. The particles do exist whether we see them with our natural unaided eyes or not.

In the same way, the spirit world exists whether we see it or not with our natural eyes or not.

Another example is that we say that the eyes are the windows of the soul. We mean that the soul and spirit of the person is the one who looks out through their eyes, hence the expression that the eyes are the windows of the soul.

Yet another example is that you know that when you sleep, you may dream yet your body is unmoving and lying still on the bed.

Yet you dream and travel and do activities in your dreams but your body is lying still on the bed and may be snoring away during all your numerous activities in your dream without getting up and leaving the comfort of your bed.

You can see that you were busy in dreams. This would be your spirit involved here. Your physical body is still on the bed. Your physical body is not affected here. Your soul is with your spirit because you are feeling emotions and feelings. These facts are, with some exceptions, the collective experience of all human beings.

So the spiritual realm exists. God exists. You exist. Fear exists as well in this spirit world.

From the spirit world, it affects and afflicts so many people to stop them fulfilling their lives and living a full life.

So, fear is a spirit that is responsible for all the fear emotions and results of what we feel and ultimately how we act.

But not all believe that the spiritual realm exists. I do not blame them. I understand their position and viewpoint.

Again, belief is a subjective thing. You either choose to believe or choose not to believe.

I choose to believe that the spiritual world exists given the fact of Jesus Christ being the only reference point for all time past and present and future and the bible being a book about Jesus.

These facts I presented above were what made me review my thinking and helped me come to consider at some level the startling fact that Jesus is who He said He is and He did what He said He was going to do.

For me, the combination of the facts above was enough evidence for me to choose to believe that Jesus is the son of God and saviour just as He said.

However, I realise that it is my choice whether to believe that Jesus is the son of God and saviour and that He is who He says He is. I then made my own free will choice to believe in Jesus and to accept him as my Lord and saviour. For me, this made total sense.

Now from a biblical point of view, dealing with fear means you are dealing with a spirit. In James 4:7 we are told how to deal with fear.

James 4:7 KJV states

"submit yourselves therefore to God. Resist the devil and he will flee from you'

This means that you have to say **NO** to fear.

You have to resist fear.

Not give in.

Is this easy? No, it is not.

Resist is both a verb an action word and a noun. Resist means to withstand, repel, counter, outlast, keep out.

This advice is further repeated in

1 Peter 5:9 KJV

"whom resist stedfast in the faith knowing the same afflictions are being accomplished by your brethren that are in the world'

We can see the advice given is to resist satan or fear. Resisting fear is the same thing as resisting satan because satan is the God of death.

The root of all fears boils down to the fear of death.

That is why the bible said in **Hebrews 2:14-15 KJV**

*"Forasmuch then as the children are partakers of flesh and blood, he also himself likewise took part of the same; that **through death he might destroy him that had the power of death, that is, the devil;** And deliver them who through **fear of death** were all their lifetime subject to bondage."*

So, Jesus's death, had the effect of destroying satan who had the power of death and delivered everyone who, because of fear, were in their entire lives subject to bondage.

This is the tool you use to resist fear. You use the name of Jesus as the weapon.

You have to be a christian to use this tool. You can't use this tool against fear because it is only given to christians.

To become a christian - you need to do the following now by praying the following prayer out loud:

1. Ask God to forgive your sins.

2. Tell God you believe that He sent Jesus to die for you and you believe that God raised Jesus up from the dead for your salvation, righteousness

3. Confess Jesus as your Lord and saviour.

4. Thank God for saving you.

Then find a good bible believing church and stay faithful.

CHAPTER 7.

POSITIVE FEAR

If you are not a christian and cannot tackle fear using the information in the previous chapter, then please read on.

You can still be helped.

Just as everything has a good and bad side, fear is not all bad. Fear has a good and bad side to it. In fact, fear can be positive or negative and has positive and negative rewards depending on what type of fear it is.

Positive fear helps to combat and constrain human excesses to achieve a quiet well ordered life and is beneficial to society. Without positive fear or respect, chaos, confusion and unrest ensues.

We need positive fear. Positive fear helps us to achieve great things, work hard, pursue our dreams and gain successes.

For example, the fear of failure is a positive fear. It is positive in that it motivates us to work hard, acquire knowledge and skill and excel and if we work hard, we achieve success and avoid failure.

Most of the wealthiest people in this world came from poverty and worked hard until they achieved fame and fortune.

People like, Steve Jobs, Oprah Winfrey, Howard Schultz of Starbucks, Ralph Lauren of the fashion world, Lakshmi Mittal, Larry Ellison of Oracle. J K Rowling, Halle Berry, Leonardo DiCaprio, Ed Sheeran, Sarah Jessica Parker, Arnold Schwarzenegger, Sir Richard Branson, Sir Alan Sugar, 50 cents, The Jackson Five, Muhammad Ali, Michael Jordan, Serena Williams, Celine Dion and so on.

They all worked hard and harder than most people will ever imagine and as a result they achieved their status.

In many interviews they have given, one recurring theme comes up again, which is, one of their main drivers and motivations to succeed was that they made up their mind never to be poor again and this fear drove them to achieve what they have achieved today.

You can see then that fear can be positive.

Positive fear is also called respect. Some of the positive fears that helps in facilitating a peaceful and quiet life for all are:

1. Fear of God

2. Respect for authorities

3. Respect for Governments

4. Respect for teachers

5. Respect for parents

6. Respect for authority figures

7. Respect for rules

8. Respect for the laws of the land.

We are to cultivate positive fear. We are to encourage others to cultivate positive fear because this leads to order, peace and creation of atmosphere for prosperity and growth.

We all need order in our lives. Not because we can't have disorder but because we have found consistently over time that disorder is not good for us and does not advance our interests or help anyone.

Disorder has no positivity in it. Rather it causes and produces even more chaos and confusion and every evil work.

We notice from our own lives that when there is peace and order, people feel safe and protected and able to go about their normal business with confidence.

We notice from the recent Covid-19 pandemic that if we did not respect the Government and its instructions, the death toll, although too high already, would have been far far higher and extremely devastating to every country of this world.

Even now, we are still following Government advice about social distancing and wearing of face masks and shields. We do this because these advices are meant to save our lives and not only our lives, the lives of others as well.

You will note that everything thrives where there is peace. Investors are happy to invest. Where there is unrest and chaos, investors flees. Businesses are shut down. Jobs lost. Lives lost and so on.

Respect for the laws of the land and authorities are all positive fears that result in good for the society and for all of us and needs to be encouraged.

This type of fear has its origins and roots in the spirit of the fear of God.

All respect for the various authorities are rooted in the belief that they were set up by God as

Romans 13:1 KJV (highlighted):

"...Let every soul be subject unto the higher powers. ___For there is no power but of God: the powers that be are ordained of God.___ *Whosoever therefore resisteth the power, resisteth the ordinance of God: and they that resist shall receive to themselves damnation. For rulers are not a terror to good works, but to the evil. Wilt thou then not be afraid of the power? do that which is good, and thou shalt have praise of the same: For he is the minister of God to thee for good. But if thou do that which is evil, be afraid; for he beareth not the sword in vain: for he is the minister of God, a revenger to execute wrath upon him that doeth evil. Wherefore ye must needs be subject, not only for wrath, but also for conscience sake. For this cause pay ye tribute also: for they are God's ministers, attending continually upon this very thing. Render therefore to all their dues: tribute to*

whom tribute is due; custom to whom custom; fear to whom fear; honour to whom honour..."

We can see that God set up the Governments and gave them their authority to act so respect for them is also respect for God with positive consequences for all of us and for us individually as well. We note that rulers are there to encourage the betterment of their citizens and many governments do that.

That is positive, isn't it? So, you can see that fear can be positive when it comes from God and not from man.

This positive fear tackles some of the personal fears that are listed on the list of fears in chapter one and can be used to diminish or eliminate some of those fears.

Yet, you have to choose positive fear. You have to make a conscious choice to chose to fear God. You have to make a conscious choice to respect the Government. You have to make a conscious choice to respect your parents. You have to make a conscious choice to do these things.

They are never automatic. The negative side of fear is automatic. You get that negative side of fear whether you like it or not. But you never get the positive side of fear automatically.

You have to **_deliberately_** and **_unemotionally_** choose positive fear.

Notice what I said. You have to deliberately and unemotionally choose positive fear everytime.

This is one way of facing your fear and winning.

This is one way to defeat negative fear. You can use this positive fear of respect for the law of the land to eliminate the fear of being attacked by criminals because the positive fear in the Governments ability to deter crime creates a safe space for you to live free from the fear of crime.

In that way, you can use positive fear to face your negative fears and win through to success and freedom. Every time.

CHAPTER 8.

NEGATIVE FEAR

We know that fear can be negative. This is by far the most experience, emotions and feelings that most people have of fear throughout the ages.

Most people describe their emotions and experiences of both positive and negative fear in its physical manifestations, emotional manifestations and mental manifestations such as:

1. Face turning ashen
2. Face turning white
3. Clammy hands
4. Cold sweats
5. Rapid blinking
6. Shaking uncontrollably
7. Licking one own lips
8. Lowering voice to a whisper
9. Beads of sweat on forehead

10. Flinching
11. Gasping
12. Whimpering
13. Staring
14. Freezing
15. Self hugging
16. Stuttering
17. Squirming
18. Tight tense shoulders
19. Holding back a cry or scream
20. Heartbeat racing
21. Dizziness
22. Pain in chest
23. A faulty sense of time
24. Sensation of doom
25. Faster heart beat
26. Cracking voice
27. Nail biting
28. Scratching skin raw
29. Tics
30. Talking to one self
31. Fainting
32. Self harm
33. Suicide attempt
34. Knocks going white

35.Eating disorders

36.Being sick

37.Many bowel movements

38.Gulping breaths rapidly

39.Flawed reasoning

40.Paranoia

41.Insomnia

42.Anger

43.Terror

44.Dread

45.Body odour

46.Running

47.Tremors in voice

48.Topic change

49.Keeping silent

50.False smile

51.Panic attacks

52.Withdrawal from others

53.Depression

54.Substance abuse and drugs

55.Hype sensitive to light, voice, smell or touch

The above list describes some of the results of positive fear and or negative fear in the human body and it is safe to say that at some point or the other we have all experienced one or more of the emotional, mental and physical manifestation of fear and we can all agree that they are not pleasant at all.

Science tells us that the fear factor will always provoke in us the instinctive feelings and emotions of fight or flight.

We know that the feelings and emotions of fight that fear provokes in us, is to prepare us to face and fight the threat.

We also know that the feelings and emotions of flight that fear produces in us, is to prepare us to run away from the threat.

I bring to your notice these two considerations.

The first consideration is that the objective of fear in these two scenarios is to preserve our lives and the ways it seeks to preserve our lives is through fighting the threat or running away from the threat.

The second consideration is that the decision to either fight or flee is taken at a subconscious level where reason or wisdom does not have the upper hand.

There, in this area of the subconscious is where you can fight your negative fears and win.

I have already indicated that fear is a spirit. I have also indicated that man is a spirit as well.

The subconscious mind is the mind of your spirit or your spirit as some writers have proffered.

To change the mind of your subconscious to tackle the unwanted negative fear is the way you face your fear and win.

Let me restate again, there is therefore no need to fear negative fear once you know what they are and why you are having these manifestations linked to the fear you are feeling at that moment.

You can then start considering how to face your fears and win.

CHAPTER 9.

FACING YOUR FEAR

To face your fear and win. You need to, first of all, gain knowledge and understanding of the fear or fears that you are dealing with.

Everyone has some fears. I would advise you write them down.

Yes. Write them all down. On a sheet of paper or in your journal.

The first step to facing any fear is to write down the exact nature of the fear. It is the first step to taking that fear captive.

Identify which type of fear we are dealing with. So far, we have seen we have positive fear and negative fear.

We have no problem with positive fear or respect. You can agree with me from your understanding of our society and the news from other countries that we need more positive respect for our governments and everything they are doing to help everyone to stay safe and not less positive respect seeing the lack of respect some people have, for governments and authority figures such as teachers.

You can agree with me that the above is true especially when you consider how in this Covid -19 pandemic, many people flouted and disobeyed the government's directions on social distancing by going to beaches, illegal raves and parties.

The actions of these few people can definitely lead to increased risk of Covid-19 for a lot of people simply because the flouters did not have any positive respect for the government, the government's directions and what the government is trying to do which was to protect us all.

We have the same scenario in schools where students disobey teachers instructions and do what they like. This shows the lack of positive respect which can be demoralising for teachers and for those who work in education and in turn affects society as the student who disobeys their teachers may likely go on and disobey their boss at their place of work and end up unemployed and possibly homeless.

No one wants to be in that position hence we all need to encourage positive respect for our governments, schools, teachers. This will bring positive dividends to everyone in society. Everyone in our society needs to have positive respect for our government and those who are in authority over us.

In facing positive fear and in dealing with positive fear, we need to encourage everyone to come on board the positive fear bandwagon and seek out others to work with us to encourage positive fear because of its importance in helping us create, strengthen and maintain our society governing structures and institutions and helps us create a better world for all.

We have seen that positive fear is good for all and should be encouraged as it has positive results. So, let define our terms.

What is a negative fear?

A negative fear is any fear that is not a positive fear and which makes the person affected fearful of hurt, injury or even death being inflicted on them by the object, the person or persons feared.

What are the roots of negative fear?

There is one spiritual root and many physical roots. The spiritual root of fear is as we stated before in **2 Timothy 1:7** which is that Fear is a spirit.

But which power controls the spirit of fear?

Satan controls the spirit of fear.

In John 10:10, KJV the bible states :

"...The thief cometh not, but for to steal, and to kill, and to destroy: I am come that they might have life, and that they might have it more abundantly..."

Notice that the three objectives of the thief who is also named the devil or satan are:

1. To steal

2. To kill

3. To destroy.

Notice that God has only two objectives:

1. To give you life

2. To give you life, more abundantly

You can tell which fear is aligned to which objectives. Positive fear is aligned to God's objectives.

Negative fear is aligned to satan or the devil's objectives. You can tell whether the fear you are experiencing is of God or from the devil according to how you feel and the emotions and physical manifestations you are experiencing.
For completeness, I need you to understand that not all fear comes from satan. Yes, a majority of fears comes from satan but that is not all.

Some negative fear can arise from us. From our own actions, thoughts and beliefs independently of the fear that comes from satan.

Whichever way they come, you have to face them by using the power of question first to determine its objectives and its current effects and manifestations.

Ask the following hard questions:

1. Is the fear stopping you from pursuing and achieving your dreams?

2. Is the fear stopping you from making progress in your life?

3. Is the fear stopping you from carrying out your job?

4. Is the fear stopping you from being comfortable and being yourself?

5. Is the fear stopping you from expressing yourself?

6. Is the fear making you regress and you feel something is being stolen from you?

7. Is the fear making you feel as if you are going to die? Be sick?

8. Is the fear making you feel that you will be destroyed? Embarrassed? Shamed?

9. Is the fear making you feel like you will be making mistakes? That all eyes are on you?

If the answers are yes, then you can be sure that you are dealing with negative fear.

Raphael's principles:
Accept that the fear you feel will never go away
completely

Negative fear never ever goes away. No matter what you do. It will never go away completely.

It is a fact that fear will always be there in your life from your birth day to your date of death and everything in-between.

However, if fear will never go away, what are you to do then?

Raphael's principles:
First, get to know and understand your fears and then face them and win.

Does this mean negative fear never ever goes away? Yes. It never goes away completely as long as you live. As long as this earth and people remain, negative fear will remain as it is so deeply embedded in our consciousness on a deeper level that you or I have ever imagined or thought.

How do you actually face your fears and win?

1. *The first step to winning against your negative fears is to accept that there is such a thing or a spirit called negative fear and accept that it never ever goes away.*

2. *The second step in dealing with negative fear requires you to recognise and understand that negative fear may mean death, depression and inability to function in life, in work, in home and in office and workplace when the fear is manifesting.*

3. *The third and very vital step in facing your fear and winning is to gain courage and face the fear you are experiencing and face its symptoms, feelings, emotions and physical manifestations on the above mentioned list.*

4. *Assess the risks to you and others should you continue to do what it is that you were doing or about to do, when the fear struck you and if the risks are low, then continue, despite your feeling the emotions of fear, to carry out the*

function, job, activity that you are doing or about to do, when fear struck you.

Yes, you have to accept that negative fear exists. You do not deny the negative fear in whatever form you have experienced it before or experiencing it now.

Acceptance of the fear means you accept that the fear experience will bring on you some or all of the symptoms, feelings, emotions and physical manifestations from any of the fear from the list of fear on the above list of fears.

Yes, you have accept that the emotions of the particular fear will many times, try to make you desperately wish to fight the threat or flee from the threat.

In fact, to accept the negative fear is a positive action because this is the very first step that will help you to face the fear and win. In fact, if you can do that, in my book you are a winner.

Why? It is because the most common reaction is for people to run away from the fear. By facing it, you are making a statement and believe you me, it gets easier, the more you face your negative fears.

This simple understanding gives us the tools that we need to face our negative fears that cripple a lot of people and emerge victorious.

Is it going to be easy? No, No and No. I can promise you it is going to be very hard and difficult. Why? It is hard because you are essentially going against your own self.

You facing yourself. Will it work?

That depends on you. As with everything in life, you are the captain of your own ship and the master of your own fate. You will be the one that will decide if this would work or not.

You will get out of this, what you put into it. There are no quick fixes or short cuts.

So then what do you have to do?

CHAPTER 10.

FACING YOUR FEARS AND WINNING

You face every negative fear and win by using the following 5 steps:

1. Identify the particular type of fear
2. Take steps to avoid the fear or do nothing
3. Prayer
4. Replace the fear
5. Reinforce the replacement of fear
6. Repeat as necessary

Why will this work?

It will work because of what I call Raphael's Law

"Every small adjustments in your subconscious mind will produce a great change in your conscious mind and change your behaviour towards your desired goals and helps you achieve them"

Simply then, to change your life. You change your thoughts. Your new thoughts will create a new you.

I will first show you the bible way of dealing with fear and then show you the secular way of dealing with fear and you will have some tools and options to choose from, to use to face your fear and win.

1. IDENTIFY THE PARTICULAR TYPE OF FEAR YOU ARE HAVING

You do so by taking the following steps:

1. Turn the light on the darkness. You do so by making use of the word of God which is light and apply them to your situation - this is using the bible's advice on dealing with fear.

2. Knowledge - get knowledge about the fear. Speak to Experts. Research the fear. Keep a journal recording how you feel and what triggers usually triggers them.

3. Reason - use reason, analyse the fears. When do they come, think about the situations and circumstances in which they arise.

4. Get benefit of experience by speaking to those who had those fears and conquered them.

5. Research the fear to know what you are dealing with.

6. People - create a support network. Speak with teachers, elders those who have gone through - how did they handle it? Have a loving non judgemental and supportive group of people to support you.

7. Removal - how can the threat causing the fear realistically be removed?

8. Endurance - can you endure the fear and come out on the other side? What is the ultimate result of the fear?

We shall examine each steps in a little more detail so you can have full understanding of the various ways you can face your fear and win.

1. Turn the light on the darkness - the bible method

To identify the fear, you need to stop and think of the list I have given you above and see if your fears are listed there. If they are, then you will have identified them.

Write them down.

The root of every kind of fear can be traced back to the fear of death and ceasing to exist. You hear people saying they wish the ground would open up and swallow them. You hear people saying they would die of embarrassment and so on and so forth.

Let us look at what the bible says about how to face your fears and win.

What is this scripture?

Proverbs 23:7 KJV
'..For as he thinketh in his heart, so is he: Eat and drink, saith he to thee; but his heart is not with thee...'

Basically, you are what you think.

Your thoughts determines who you are and your thought determines your behaviour.

If you change your thoughts, you will change your behaviour which will change your life because you will get different results and hopefully better outcome because you will be reacting differently to fears, different from how you used to respond previously.

This change of thoughts and thinking is at the root of cognitive behavioural psychology and complementary therapies such as meditations and other forms of cognitive therapies.

If you think about it, Fear is simply an accumulation of fear thoughts that has overpowered the person's mind and is forcing a negative emotional response from the person towards the object of their fears.

If you change those thoughts - not wait for someone to change them for you - you will see your thoughts changed and your behaviour will change and people will respond differently to your different behaviour and you have faced your fear and won.

This is one of the ways, you can face your fear and win.

Why is the bible information so important?

Well, let us start with considering why the bible is so important.

1 John 1:5 KJV

"...This then is the message which we have heard of him, and declare unto you, that <u>God is light,</u> and in him is no darkness at all..."

Note it says that God is LIGHT.
This means that all light proceeds from God. So when you need light on any subject matter, you go to God to give you light on that subject matter.

Interestingly the first act of creation in the book of Genesis 1:3 is that God created light. Furthermore, the scripture verse:

Psalm 119:130 NJKV
"...The entrance of Your words gives <u>light</u>; It gives understanding to the simple..."

So, the words of God gives light.

That's because God is light.

So, God is light and His words are light and brings light into every situation including the situations of fear. As we have previously stated, negative fears are darkness and here we have light that can light up that darkness so we are enabled to see what is in that darkness that is making us afraid and unable to function to the best of our abilities.

Now we have light upon this issue of fear.

So, what is God's attitude towards negative fear?

For starters, God does not fear anyone. God has no respect or fear for anyone. Now, God's ability and capability is such even if you add all 7 billion people in this world plus all the billions that have existed in this earth before us and multiply them with all the powers of the dinosaurs and spirits, with all our powers, abilities and capabilities, all put together will amount to nothing before God's omnipotent power and greatness.

This fact is confirmed by Daniel 4:35

Daniel 4:35 KJV
"...all the peoples of the earth are reputed as nothing..."

You can now understand why God is not afraid of us or any thing.

What is God's solution?

God's attitude towards you having negative fear is to say to you these light filled words:

Isaiah 35:4 New Living Translation

"...Say to those with fearful hearts, "Be strong, and <u>do not fear</u>, for your God is coming to destroy your enemies. He is coming to save you..."

God says to you regarding fear: **Be Strong. Do not be afraid of fear.**

God repeats this same message in Isaiah 41:23 The Good News translation

Isaiah 41:23 Good News translation

"...The LORD says, "Small and weak as you are, Israel, <u>don't be afraid;</u> I will help you. I, the

holy God of Israel, am the one who saves you..."

Here we see this message repeated again: **Do not be afraid of fear.**

Then in Acts 18:9 NKJV, God spoke to Paul saying

Acts 18:9 New King James Version

"...Now the Lord spoke to Paul in the night by a vision, "<u>Do not be afraid,</u> but speak, and do not keep silent..."

Yet, again we see the same message from God: <u>**Do not be afraid of fear.**</u>

What reason does God give you, for you to use to face your fear and win?

The reason is that God is with you.

But How?

It means that He is in some way with you even if you do not see Him or touch Him or even aware that He is still with you.

God would not lie about this, would He? I don't think so. If God is not afraid of anyone because He is more powerful than everyone added together, then He has no reason to lie and He does not need to lie either.

He says here:

Isaiah 41:10
"...Do not fear for I am with you..."

Again, He repeats it here:

Matthew 28: 20
"...Behold I am with you even to the end of the age..."

You can readily see that in all three scriptures in different eras of the bible, to different audiences, God is emphasising the point that you should not be afraid.

You can say it this way. Light says to you. Do not be afraid of darkness.

He is emphasising the fact that you are not to be afraid because He is with you to help you and save you.

It works if you believe it.

To believe it, you have to constantly ensure you think these thoughts over and over and over again for thousands of times - ***that God is with me so I am not going to be afraid of fear***.

You speak those words and you make sure you think on them over and over and over and over and over again and then again. Thousands of times over.

At some point during you doing the above, your subconscious or your spirit will receive this information and your life will be transformed straightaway.

How does this work? I don't know. But does it work? I would say from from personal experience, that it worked for me and still working for me.

The fact is that you have to work at it over and over and never give up, because God's words, that He was with me, for me, was the catalyst for me facing my fears and winning.

Once I realised that God is with me, this gave me courage and strength to face my fears because I reasoned that God would not be with me only to mock me and stand by and watch me whilst I struggled.

I believed if He was with me, I do not need to fear any more because I had access to His strength and anything I was afraid would not be able to attack me or cause me any problem since God would be able to deal with them.

This meant that I received the courage and confidence to face my fears and win.

These experiences taught me that the number one key to facing your fears and winning is the combination of courage and confidence.

You have to have the courage and confidence in God and in God's words, to face your fear and it is that confidence and courage in God's words and promises that gives you the victory over fear in the bible method.

Will it work for you?

Absolutely.

Why?

The reason why it will work for you is that God is no respecter of persons.

Acts 10:34 puts it this way

Acts 10:34 New Living Translation
'...Then Peter replied, I see very clearly that God shows no favouritism..."

God does not show favouritism. He extends the same promise to you and to all 7 billion people in the world.

Further, God loves you and his promises to you are based on His everlasting love for you.

Jeremiah 31:3 ESV - I have loved you with an everlasting love therefore I have continued my faithfulness to you.

And God goes further to show and demonstrate that love for you and me by sending Jesus to die for the world.

John 3:16 - For God so loved the world that He gave his one and only Son that whoever believes in him shall not perish but shall have eternal life.

That's why it will work for you. God is invested in you becoming the person He has created you to be, so that the world will be made better because you carry a gift and an ability that the world needs.

2. Knowledge

Remember that we said that the first thing to defeat your fears is to accept them. To accept them is to have willingness to live with them and know them.

How do you know about your fears?

You need to get knowledge and more knowledge about your fears. This knowledge may take on many forms. It could be knowledge about yourself.

Knowledge of how you came to have these fears.

You have to start with yourself. You have to ask yourself questions along the lines of the very first memory of your fears. When did it first begin? Where did it first happen? What was the circumstances when it happened. What feeling and emotions did they cause you at the beginning?

Are they causing the same emotions and feelings for you now? What are your triggers? When are your triggers triggered? Really, at this stage, you want to collect as much information about your fears as you possibly can. Research the fear. What does others say about it. Do other people have it? Is there a support group?

The more you know of your fears the more you are able to know your enemy and then it is during this seeking for a clear knowledge of what you are dealing with, that sometimes the answers emerges.

You will need to have a journal and be diligent in recording your experiences and emotions. You are doing this because it is a very valuable tool that would give you or any person helping you to gain a good picture of the severity or otherwise of your fears and when they attack you the most and what your triggers are.

You can then speak with an expert in this area and they would be able to educate you on the subject of your fears and give you the benefit of their experience and knowledge in the subject of your unique fears.

The information gathered will then enable you to pinpoint the exact issues and fears you wish to face and win. A word of caution, if you have more than one fear as it is the case for all of us. It is not a case of simply having a fear. Many of us have fears.

It is sensible to address one issue of fear at a time. Do not try to do too many at a time as that will only make things worse and you won't be able to have any success on them.

The sensible course of action is to just do one fear at a time and concentrate on winning that and then go on to the next and the next.

Each time, you will find that your confidence in the face of that fear will grow and that fear will just shrink enough for you to operate at the level you have always desired to but which your fears has been stopping you.

3. Reasonings

In facing your fears and winning. Reasoning is one of your biggest allies needed for you to succeed.

Reason is your ability to process information logically and arrive at conclusions that fits the facts and which any other person with their reasoning faculties are able to follow your reason and arrive at the same conclusions. Everybody reasons. Some people reason more than other people for various reasons such as their jobs, situation in life etc etc but everyone at some level can reason or process information.

Reasoning is another way of putting a search light on the fears and work out a way to face them and win.

A big secret I will reveal to you. This secret is that Fears are themselves afraid of being analysed.

Fears are afraid that their true nature will be found out once they are analysed and put under the microscope.

There are many ways to analyse the fears. One is to take the facts that you established by your journal and sit down and look at them carefully. Do you notice a pattern?

Once you see the pattern. Apply your reasoning abilities to the problem and to the fears. Reason it out.

To help you, you can create a checklist of 'what' 'why' and 'who' questions designed to tease out the fear.

I call them my Nando's questions. I base them on their extra hot, hot and mild seasonings. The extra hot questions are the deep currents of emotions. The hot questions are in-between the deep currents of emotions and the surface current of emotions. The mild are the surface currents.

1. What if my fears came true?(extra hot question)

2. What is this fear costing me potentially? (extra hot question)

3. Am I willing to pay the price of what it is going to cost me? (extra hot question)

4. What has this fear costed me in the past? (hot question)

162

5. What is this fear likely to cost me in the future ? (extra hot question)

6. What am I afraid of - potentially? (hot question)

7. What am I afraid of - actually? (extra hot question)

8. What happened when I was afraid like this before? (hot question)

9. Do I have any reasonable explanation for what happened when I was afraid like this before? (hot question)

10. What is the very worst that could happen to me with this fear, that I am feeling right now? (extra hot question)

11. What would be the most realistic bad things that will happen to me with this fear I am feeling right now? (hot question)

12. What would be the least horrible things that will happen to me with this fear I am feeling right now? (mild question)

Using the above checklist, for example, many many years ago, before speaking to a Judge in court on behalf of clients, right in the beginning of his career as a lawyer, a black lawyer in United States of America would get very nervous as the time for him to speak to the court came for him to conduct his clients case. It would feel to him as if it is a doomsday clock of judgement and he would feel panicked and his mind will then go blank especially if it was before judges that he knew to be harsh judges.

To combat this fear, he started to keep a journal of these happenings and would sit down at the end of the trial to analyse what had happened and when he examined his journal, he found out the following:

1. He was afraid and flustered because he was expecting to get roasted by the Judge - even though, there was no reason to receive a

roasting from the judge because be was always well prepared. But as you will already know from the information given in this book, fear can be unreasonable and have no basis in reality but nevertheless can manifest inexplicably.

2. This roasting will make him look foolish and incompetent and then...

3. His clients would be disappointed in him and then...

4. He would lose the case even though he had the better case to achieve a win for his client and ...

5. Even if he could win his case, but his face did not fit in the court because of the colour of his skin.

Did the above happen? Did they all come true? Of course, no.

Did some of them come to pass? Absolutely, yes!

Did he get roasted by the Judge? Yes. sometimes.

Did his face not fit in the court because of the colour of his skin? Yes, sometimes.

Did the roasting make him look foolish and incompetent? No. It did not.

Using this information, he was able to respond and keep his cool inside the court under pressure and later it transpired that the judge was testing his clients case to point its weaknesses and not directly undermining him but thankfully, the weaknesses (every case has weakness - no case is 100% perfect) were not enough to stop him from winning his cases.

But he also discovered something else that he was not expecting. He found out if he was genuinely polite, pleasant and helpful to everyone no matter their position whether they are the cleaners or the court staff in the courts, he received help and assistance and the above fears, that he had, did not happen or come to pass as much.

But he also discovered something else, there are harsh Judges. But there are mostly fair Judges and

Judges are also human beings like him, you and me.

He could then see that the reason for him feeling fearful, nervous and anxious in his first few cases was because of a combination of his fears, harsh judges, opponents, hard cases.

Once he understood these simple facts, he was able to face his fears and win.

The above is a true and real experience of some people that I have taught this method to and these people are from all races and nationalities and they have succeeded using the methods I have outlined in this book.

The lesson I am teaching you to never to judge a book by its cover and never to react to appearances of fear without subjecting it to analyses and reasoning before being able to find a solution that enables you to manage the situation.

4. Get the benefit of experienced people

Experience is the best teacher they say.

Nowhere is more true than in this situation. You need to seek out people with experience in dealing with the type of fears you wish to confront. You need people who have had the fears themselves as they know what the fears can do and they will appreciate how you feel and the challenges you are going through.

You need to speak to a wide range of people, teachers and people who have undergone the same type of fear as you and have tools to manage them or keep themselves and their life unaffected by the fear and use the knowledge you have gleaned from them to face your fear and win.

They would be able to give you guidance of what is working for them, what has worked for them in the past and why. They would be able to even point you to certain doctors, psychologists who they have success in treating the condition.

The most important thing here is to realise that you are not alone. You are not a freak and in fact, you are quite normal. There are others like you.

The understanding that you are not alone is very empowering. It means that you are in a community and which means that if it is a sickness, there would be resources available for research into finding a cure or using cognitive behavioural tools to face those fears and come out a winner.

You may start looking for experienced people using your local Doctors surgery. Your Doctor would be able to have resources to point you in the direction of experienced people, organisations and groups.

You can also make enquiries at your local councils and churches or the internet.

You can then use the help that you receive to face your fears and win.

5. Research the fear

You need to do your own research on your fear to know what you are dealing with before you can then face your fears and win. You need to look for information about your fear through books, internet, doctors surgery, personal experiences and get as much as you can.

You need to know what it is that you are dealing with and the more thorough your research is, the more you will feel confident to devise a way that you can adopt to face the fear and win.

Once you have done enough research, you can then use the results of your research to face the fears and win.

6. Support network

Do you have a support network?

Who has your back when the worst happens? Do you have a safe place? Who are your support systems? Do you even have a support system?

We all need a support network. People around us who can help us when we are at the end of our tether. When we cannot help ourselves.

You need people who are non judgemental, accepting of you and your fears and not going to look down on you and make you feel as if you are a freak for having these fears.

We need these kind of people who may or not be our own family members? They may or may not be our friends who can hep us to be objective and be able to cope with the disasters and problems of life.

Also, ensure you have a safe place to go when you are unable to function because of fear.
You can also join groups specialising in dealing with that fear and they can help and support you through dealing with your fear.

You have to ask yourself these difficult and hard questions about your support network because you need them.

If you do not have these networks, make it your top priority to create one by repairing old relationships that has wounded you but you still care for them. You can explore healing these old wounds with loved ones through forgiveness.

You could also set about making new friends. There are people like you out there who are looking for new genuine friends.

Start and don't give up until you succeed. You can take up a new hobby and through your hobby and interests you can meet new people.

7. Removal

In doing your research, you have to give thought to how can the fear be removed. You may have to start by asking yourself the very difficult question of whether the fear can be removed.

This question may be changed to, is the removal going to be by eliminating the threat causing the fear? What do I mean by the threat causing the fear. Let's take one of the fears listed in the list of fears in chapter one of this book. Let's take, for example, the fear of water.

One way to remove this fear is to not go into any water. Not to swim in any body of water as long as you live. By not swimming in any water and not going into any water, you have, by so doing, eliminated the fear by removing yourself from every water.

Is this possible in your case? Can you remove that fear? That is one way of face the fear and winning.

But if you have a dream of swimming for exercise, you could face the fear by starting to learn how to swim and take baby steps towards that.

This option will enable you master your fear of swimming in water. And you still have the option of removal of the fear by never swimming or going near water.

8. Endurance

The other option that many people have used and are still using is the option of endurance.

Endurance means enduring the fear, enduring its emotional upheavals, pulls and idiosyncrasies and staying with the endurance until you no longer have to endure or you have found another way to handle the fear.

The requirement for endurance may typically arise where there is no other option or when you need to achieve or accomplish certain matters and you have to do so despite your fears.

For example, you are at work and your boss asks you to drive over to another company and pick up a delivery for him and bring it back to the office.

You have a fear of driving.

Here, you are in a difficult position. Let's say you did not tell them that you cannot drive or that you have a fear of driving.

On the other hand, you do not want to lose your job or let your boss down. You may then reason it that it is not a far distance to drive to. You may say, it would not take you long to drive there and drive back.

You can then say that even though you fear driving, because of what is at stake, you will confront your fears by enduring them throughout the time it will take you to drive to pick up the delivery and bring them back to your boss.

You will then go to your car or the company car and drive to the place of collection. Whilst you are driving, you are enduring the fear. Many times, you just want to pull over and run away from the car or you want to call your partner or someone you know and who knows about your fears to come and drive the car for you.

If there is no one you may continue to endure your fear with clenched teeth, white knuckles and beads of sweat coming down your forehead but you still continue to endure and you arrived at the place of collection and collect everything you were asked to

175

collect and then you may wait for several minutes to rest and prepare yourself for your next ordeal.

When you are ready, you get into the car and drive back to your place of work feeling sick to your stomach, emotional and sweaty. You grit your teeth and endure the drive until you arrive back at your place of work and then after delivering the package, you go into the toilet and throw up or take medication or calming yourself down through your breathing techniques.

You see that you have faced the fear of driving and won. But the way you used to win has exerted a cost from you but you were able to endure the fear and still succeed.

What is required for this method to succeed is that you have an important objective that the consequences of the failure to achieve that objective far outweighs the failure that may result by giving into that fear in the first place.

You have to ascertain that important objectives and rank them in higher priority than the consequences of giving into that fear.

Once you have done so, you will find that you will then be properly motivated to put into effect the method of endurance and use this method to face the fear and win.

Many fears can be faced through this method of endurance successfully and result in many wins for you.

2. TAKE STEPS TO AVOID THE FEAR OR DO NOTHING

As we have seen in list of fears that I set out earlier, not all fears are deeply entrenched and it is possible to live with some types of fear without it being a big deal.

We have to recognise that doing nothing is an option and an option that somebody may choose.

This may be that the work and effort required to be put in to face their fears are simply too much for you.

It may be that you have so many things going on and you cannot afford to devote any time and your resources to facing your fears so you may think to yourself "I cannot be bothered"

This is an option you have and if you feel you honestly are exhausted and there is no more energy within you to summon to help you face your fear and win, then you will, by default, will have chosen the option of doing nothing.

What will be the result of doing nothing?

Nothing!

You will have the same issues and same fears and you are no more nearer to facing them and winning.

Obviously, I encourage you to face the fears and win because you can and you are able to, no matter the length of time it may take you before you start to see the fruits of your efforts.

Even with this length of time and the effort required, is it absolutely worth it?

Yes, it is worth it.

It is worth you making sustained efforts to face your fears and win. It is worth it because you will be making an investment in yourself and gain a better you and a more positive future in which you realise your dreams and be all you were meant to be.

But if you do not wish to make the effort, or cannot for any reason make the effort, no one will judge you or class you as a failure because no one is perfect.

But having said that, the good thing about these principles are that you can always come back at some point to them and if you feel you are in a better place to work on them then, then you can do so, at that time.

We have to recognise that the life span of us mortals is not very long. So, you can think of it in this way - should I spend most of my time trying to change my thoughts and if I am not successful and if I do not have time to do the work required to change my thoughts and my behaviour then maybe I should not even try.

Or, you may have tried everything and nothing has worked for you and you have given up.

Well, the steps to avoid the fear is for you, it is practical and you probably are already doing it but not realising it.

It will work so long as you are prepared to make some adjustments to your life and your day to day expectations. You have a choice, you can face those fears and use your own routines and habits to face them or avoid them altogether.

What does it mean to avoid the fear?

It means that you take every step possible to avoid having to face them. For example, one of the fears I listed in the small list of fears earlier on, is the fear of flying. This is perfectly easy to avoid. For example, If you are travelling to another country, you can travel by car or by sea. If you do so, you will avoid having to travel by air so you are not exposed to your fear of flying.

Let us take Mr A for example, who has a fear of flying and has been through many therapies and none has worked and he has given up hope. Well, he still has the choice of choosing to work out ways of avoiding the fear.

It means that he can face his fears by first acknowledging that he is afraid. That is, He says, I have a fear of flying. Once, he has acknowledged the fear. He can then face the fear by saying I cannot get rid of it so I will manage it by finding ways to avoid it and live a perfectly normal as possible life for the rest of my days.

So, say Mr A, who lives in England wants to go on holiday to Paris, France. Flying to Paris is quick but that is out of the question.

So Mr A has options. He can go by bus, train or by ferry. These will take more time but that is the cost of avoiding the fears.

So, avoiding your fears will always cost you. It may cost you time, more money and more investment.

Either way, it will cost you but it is still better to pay these costs than to be totally defeated by the fears and not being able to enjoy life and achieve your dreams and die unfulfilled.

So, so long as Mr A, plans ahead in good time, he is able to go on holiday to Paris and have an enjoyable time.

Let us look at another example. Say Ms B has a fear of cooking. Now, the way to avoid this fear is to go out to eat or order from just eat restaurants and they can have a delicious meal. They can also buy ready made meals from the supermarkets.

But, there is a cost of avoidance. This cost is the amount of money she would have to spend on food depending on her desires and what she would like to eat.

So, we can see that it is quite possible to avoid some fears and still live a perfectly normal life. It is not the best option but it is a realistic option that is available to everyone.

There are some fears that this option of avoidance will not work on and you will have to confront them so it is best to learn the following four ways to face your fears and win - just in case you need them.

2. PRAYER

Prayer is one of the most powerful way to face your fears and win.

What is prayer?

Prayer is any form of words made to a higher invisible supernatural and powerful being requesting them to help and assist the person praying in whatever request they make.

Majority of people pray. The being they pray to are different depending on their culture and upbringing.
So for example, you have a person who is afraid of driving on the motorways but they need to go on a journey where they cannot avoid the motorways, using this technique, they start to pray for their journey to have a safe journey and then they pray all the way to their destination.

They get there safely.

They have faced their fear of driving on the motorway with prayers and have won.

Another example is where a child learns to drive and they drive off to see their friends. One parent would start to pray for their child journey and safety and only stop when the child returns home safely.

You see, prayer does have the power to help you face your fears and win.

3. REPLACE THE FEAR

This is a very effective way to face the fear and win.

The science behind this is what I call thought replacement method.

As we have seen earlier, thoughts comes to us from all sides and on all different subject matter. So, after you have done the diagnostics I advised in the section of identifying your fears and you now know your fears then you can easily identify the thoughts relating to that fear.

You will know them because birds of the same feather flock together. The thoughts relating to that fear are all clustered together

So, let's illustrate.

Suppose Mr B has a fear of heights. This means that whenever he sees anything that resembles heights anywhere, he will feel fear and show some of the symptoms and the emotions as I have touched upon earlier.

Now, if we go deeper, we find that the fear of heights is an aggregate of every thought that Mr B has had in relation to heights and the dangers therein.

What does Mr B do?

The first thing is to recognise these thoughts and take them captive. In other words, he becomes aware of these thoughts coming into his mind and he makes sure that he is alert to any time those thoughts come.

Once he becomes aware, then he moves on to take those thoughts captive. You see those thoughts are in Mr B's mind so he has some control over them.

In **2 Corinthians 10:5** The bible instructs us to take every thought captive and to make those thoughts obey Christ. The law of Christ is the law of love.
Love God and Love your neighbour as yourself.

Now the law is that you love your neighbour however, you are to love yourself. Yes, you are to love yourself. Why? Your love for yourself is going to be the same love you will use to love your neighbour.

So, if you do not love yourself, how will you love others? How do you love yourself?

You first accept yourself, warts and all as being lovable. As being worthy of love.

How do you do this?

Start to compliment yourself. Start to look for the best in yourself. Be diligent and persistent. It is a very very slow process.

Why?

You are re programming your subconscious mind. The subconscious takes ages to accept the information but once it does, change happens, permanently.

So be patient. Be patient. I say it again, be patient with your self.
Ok?
Then you start to replace those negative thoughts of fear with positive thoughts.

Example. Remember Mr B with the fear of heights? So, he starts by becoming aware of any fear related thoughts of heights. Say, a thought comes as he does up a lift to the 11th floor saying "you are going to die"

He takes this thought captive to the law of Christ which is the Law of Love.

Is it lovely to tell himself who he is supposed to love that he is going to die? He now challenges this thought - that this thought is not a thought that is on the law of Christ. It is not lovely.

What does Mr B do? He replaces this thought or challenges this thought with the thought that ' the building is safe. This building has passed several planning hurdles before being built. It would have passed building safety regulations and fire safety inspections, so it is safe for me and I will be safe.

Now, Mr B has now challenged the thought with the truth and the facts. Now, he can go ahead and replace the thought with the thought I am going to be safe.

This accords with the law of Christ because his being safe is a form of loving himself which he has to do before he can love others as himself.

Another way he can take the thought captive or replace the thoughts is to use affirmations or scriptures.

Affirmations are statements of positivity that are meaningful to the individual. Mr B can make up his affirmation based on scriptures or his goals and objectives.

As a person thinks so is he or she. (Proverbs 23:7) Become aware of what you are thinking of and start to replace those thoughts with facts and then act on those facts and this will renew your mind and transform you.

What sort of thoughts can you use to replace fear thoughts? What should your thoughts consist of? What is the ideal thoughts you should be thinking of?

Philippians 4:8 lists these thoughts:

1. Whatever is true

2. Whatever is noble

3. Whatever is right

4. Whatever that is pure

5. Whatever is lovely

6. Whatever is admirable

7. Whatever is excellent

8. Whatever is praiseworthy

These are the thoughts you need to use to replace every negative, evil thoughts you may encounter in your thinking.

4. REINFORCE THE REPLACEMENT OF THE FEAR THOUGHT

Mr B must continue to reinforce the replacement of the fear thoughts and associated thoughts. It is said that it takes 21 days to form a new habit. Mr B has to reinforce his new positive thoughts thousands of times before the subconscious will take that thought and make the great change that Mr B has been wanting. This change will transform Mr. B.

The reinforcement can be make sure you discuss with a friend or support system you have.

It could be keeping a journal to record your progress.

It takes patience to stick at it for thousands of times before it happens in an instant.

It takes that amount of time for it to penetrate into your subconscious and once it is received by your subconscious then the changes are effected instantly and you are transformed.

Now, be prepared for failure but work towards success. You may fail a few or a lot of times but the most important thing is to never ever give up but stick at it.

Stick at it with a bull dog mentality and you will surely face your fears and come out a winner!

5. REPEAT AS NECESSARY

Once, you have mastered the above steps, go over them again and again. Usually, I advise doing it first thing in the morning and the last thing at night before you sleep.

The reason is that first thing in the morning makes you to consciously think of what you are trying to achieve and focuses your attention on the task at hand.

The last thing at night helps you to review what you have learnt about your journey that day in learning how your thoughts have flowed and will help you become more aware of your own thoughts and you will learn more about yourself.

Go over them carefully and ponder on them and then repeat the process again and again until you succeed.

Failure will happen but don't let it bother you. Every invention went through rejection and failure thousands of times before they got it right finally.

Thomas Edison who invented the light bulb said it took him 1000 attempts before he was successful. They asked him the question why he failed 1000 times before he got it right?

He replied that the light bulb was an invention that had 1000 steps. Take a tip from Edison and never give up and practice over and over and over again thousands of times.

At a certain point in the thousands of times you are practicing thought replacement and meditation, the information you are meditating upon will be communicated to your subconscious mind or your spirit and your mind will be renewed and then your whole behaviour will change and you will achieve your objective and realise your dreams.

If this book has helped you even one bit, please could I ask you for a small favour? Please consider going to any orphanage, hospitals and homeless charities near where you live and help the orphans, the sick, the disabled, the homeless with food, clothing and finances if you are able to and help make this world a better place for those less fortunate.

Thank you!

ABOUT THE AUTHOR

Raphael Christopher is a Pastor, Teacher, Author, Counsellor and Humanitarian with a keen interest in humanitarian matters and empowerment of all mankind to be safe, succeed and achieve their full potential to make the world a better place for everyone.

Printed in Great Britain
by Amazon